THE ACCIDENTAL DIPLOMAT

THE ACCIDENTAL DIPLOMAT

Adventures in the Foreign Office

Paul Knott

Scratching Shed Publishing Ltd

'Armed with five 'O' Levels and a fascination for other countries, Paul Knott managed to secure a job as a Foreign Office diplomat. This allowed him to export his typical Hull sense of humour to parts of the world where laughter was an endangered emotion. This is a book that achieves the rare combination of being instructive and funny."

Rt. Hon. Alan Johnson MP

'An unexpectedly engrossing read about the adventures of an unlikely diplomat. Paul is a smart Yorkshire boy made good - if you count Humberside as part of Yorkshire. He is now an excellent writer on foreign affairs, whose insights from his Foreign Office career frequently put him ahead of the pack.'

James Brown, Editor-in-Chief, Sabotage Times

'The hilarious and engrossing tale of how one ordinary bloke from Hull stumbled onto the world political stage by accident...'

Russ Litten, Author of
Scream if You Want to Go Faster
and Swear Down

Typeset in Warnock Pro Semi Bold and Palatino
Printed and bound in the United Kingdom by
Charlesworth Press, Flanshaw Way, Flanshaw Lane,
Wakefield, WF2 9LP

To my lovely children, so that one day you will read this and understand what Daice used to do before he started hanging around the house so much.

With love and thanks to Dad for giving me determination, Mum for making me a reader and Mwana for making this book, and so much else that matters, happen.

Acknowledgements

MANY outstanding people have contributed to the writing of this book, either directly or through their influence on the story and the person recounting it.

I must thank my friends in Her Majesty's Diplomatic Service for all of the laughs, support and comradeship you have given me over the years. You know who you are and some of you will recognise yourselves in the following pages. But I hope that I have disguised your identities well enough to ensure that your personnel and security officers do not.

Thanks too to the people and bar staff in all of the countries to which I have been posted for making it such an enjoyable and informative ride. Most of all, for teaching me that we are all much more alike than we are different: the mundane yet most profound truth I learnt during my years travelling the world.

Plenty of credit for the finished product should go to Phil Caplan and Tony Hannan at Scratching Shed Publishing. Tony created the striking design. Phil did an excellent job of sharpening my prose and bringing focus to my rambles down memory lane. He also provided wise counsel throughout the writing and publishing process.

I am grateful to Tina Leggett for her terrific help in reading and advising on the manuscript at an earlier stage.

My mighty mother-in-law, Dr Rita Lugogo, performed a similar sterling service. She and my greatly missed father-in-law, Professor Juma Lugogo, have taught me much about the world and how to be a force for good in it. I am grateful to them for welcoming me so warmly into their family.

In memory of my beloved grandparents, Walter and Violet Knott, and William and Beatrice Norton, and my 'Uncle Les', Leslie Englestown. The greatest generation and my absolute heroes. Thank you for teaching me and Tony how to be decent people without us noticing that you were doing anything more than caring for and having fun with us.

Thanks to my brother Tony Knott for visiting me in the places that were not in the holiday brochures. You will always have first claim on the spare room.

To my Mum, Gillian, and Dad, Peter: I am supposed to be a writer now but can hardly find the words adequate to express my gratitude for the fantastic childhood and upbringing you gave us and for everything that you continue to do. I realise that it must have been tough at times and that what you gave us is priceless. I love you both.

Thank you to my lovely kids for the happiness you bring me and the privilege of watching you grow.

Last but a long, long way from least, I thank my wonderful wife, Mwana Lugogo, for agreeing to share her life with me and for her love, without which many of the most important parts of my life would not exist.

You are my inspiration.

Contents

1. Why me?

A FORMER Soviet airbase in Dnipropetrovsk; one of the coldest, most desolate locations in the world. The perfect place to get rid of a diplomat.

Who would ever know? The crisp deep snow would hide all traces and news of any disappearance would travel slowly from such a distant outpost, if at all.

I pulled up the collar on my trenchcoat and thrust my hands deep inside my pockets, the sub-zero temperatures in stark contrast to my sweaty palms. What the hell was I doing here, disembarking from an Ukranian military jet with a delegation of NATO Ambassadors, MiG fighters taking off all around us? How long before the so-called guard next to me - tall, angular, with a box-shaped head and impervious to the chill - put his menacing PK machine gun to my neck and bundled this Western interloper from his runway?

My head, encased in a Cossack hat, began to throb viciously, the veins in my temples standing proud under the skin as my breath crystallised in front of me. I desperately hoped that a Bond girl in little more than a fur coat would slink from the shadowy hanger and say: *'Zo, Meester Knott, ve have been expecting you.'* It must have been her night off.

My wild imaginings aside, this is not how it actually happened of course. Genuine working life in the Foreign Office and the fictional tales of Ian Fleming's 007 inhabit parallel universes. But with the screech of aero-engines almost ear-splitting, I did wonder, not for the first time, how an ordinary bloke from Hull had got here.

This is not one of those conventional stories about a driven, working-class lad burning to break the chains of his origins and make it in the big, wide world. My joining Her Majesty's Diplomatic Service was not a lifelong ambition, nor was my career a carefully plotted rise to Ambassador.

Diplomacy did not feature on the radar screen of young people from my background. I was a pupil of South Holderness School - a large, bog-standard comprehensive. My grandfathers were unskilled factory workers. One of my grandmas worked in a bread factory, the other baked exclusively for us in the tiny kitchen of her council house.

Dad nudged us up the scale by working all hours to establish a small used car business. And Mum's break from battling to keep everything on track at home was a Saturday job at British Home Stores. All of their efforts, though, meant that my brother and I never wanted for anything. Most of all, we received the priceless gift of a happy, secure and well-grounded childhood.

Apart from having a loving family there, I had no great desire to get away permanently from Hull either. It is a tough place in some respects and geographically isolated, but the port city has a distinctive history, character and wit that is ingrained in me. I had lived there all my life, loved the place and still do.

But when I left school at the fag-end of Thatcherism in the late 1980s, Hull was not exactly bursting with employment options. The long recession had arrived there earlier than the rest of the country, principally with the decline of the fishing industry in the 1970s and, to those outside, the curiously-named 'cod wars'. Aspirations for most of my cohort climbed no higher than getting anything that paid a liveable wage. Job satisfaction and excitement were not on the agenda.

My broad mental horizons were perhaps the only thing that distinguished me from my contemporaries. I had been fascinated by the world from an early age. The wanderlust was fuelled by the war stories of my grandfathers and great uncle, the tales of seamen that are part of a port's fabric, and family holidays on the Costa del Sol. I vividly recall spending hours poring over my treasured atlas, wondering what places were like beyond the bare details of their geography. How did they look, sound and feel? What went on there and what were the people like? This background may not have matched the cosmopolitan upbringing and Oxbridge education of the traditional Diplomatic Service recruit. But it was enough to guarantee that a leaflet that appeared on the Careers Office' shelves one day would grab my attention.

After a brief flirtation with the Army and Navy Recruitment Centre (the armed forces, not the department store), I spent a lot of time in the Careers Office during my two years at Hull College of Further Education. Apart from being somewhere warm to sit until the pub opened, it was the best place to pursue a job with travel that did not involve getting shot at. I applied for numerous vacancies in glamorous locations such as Northampton and Droitwich Spa. But even these diverse offerings could not match the attraction of working in far flung British Embassies described in the flyer about Her Majesty's Diplomatic Service. Better still, and contrary to popular perception, there was no indication that being an Old Etonian with several generations of relatives in the Service was necessary. Instead, five O' Levels and a willingness to pack a suitcase would suffice.

As with many of the job applications I made, I had no great expectations that my bid for entry into the Diplomatic Service would succeed. Even ordinary vacancies at that time often attracted hundreds of applicants and this one seemed to be the longest of long shots. My low expectations appeared to have been met when I heard nothing from the Foreign Office for several months.

My parents, thankfully - with hindsight, although I was not particularly grateful at the time - were not the kind of people to let me hang around until a suitably attractive offer turned up. They prodded me to accept a job as a 'gofer' for a haulage company on Hull's King George Dock. Apart from starting work at six in the morning, seven days a week, for a wage of sixty-five pounds, this role meant sitting in a freezing Portakabin, heated only by the lorry exhaust fumes wafting in from the road. I did try to warm the place up a bit on my first day. As was tradition, the first act of my working life was to make a cup of tea for everyone in the office. This went well apart from my dropping the still plugged-in power cord from the kettle into a half-eaten Pot Noodle in the bin and setting fire to the kitchen.

In fairness, life on the docks was fun. My colleagues were great and some of the dockers and lorry drivers had personalities as big as the bacon sandwiches in the café. The ships, when you could see them through the fog, offered the whiff of foreign travel too. On several occasions I almost earned a free trip to Rotterdam by getting locked in the hold of the ferry whilst posting 'hazardous material' stickers on trucks just before sailing time. Two of us even got a fortnightly excursion to Teesport in Middlesbrough, where we hung around waiting for the ship to arrive whilst eating fish and chips and watching dockers race new Nissans around the no-man's land between the ICI chemicals plant and Hartlepool nuclear power station.

Engrossed in all of this glitz, I had more or less forgotten about my Foreign Office application when suddenly, in quick succession, I was called to interview, accepted and instructed to apply for security clearance before starting work in London. The vetting procedure involved a security officer visiting my home, school, workplace and nominated referees to dig for evidence of extremist political leanings, substance abuse and such like.

As an indication of the social circles from which the Diplomatic Service usually recruited, the request for references suggested nominating someone in authority who knew you well such as your MP, Vicar or a senior military officer, on the apparent assumption that it was absolutely normal to be closely acquainted with such people. The nearest I could get was our much-loved family friend, Gordon Keyworth, on the grounds that he was a part-time fireman.

My other referee was my boss on the docks, Roy Simpson. He told me that he had given me a glowing reference in the hope of getting rid of me whilst he was still alive and his office was still standing. Whatever the motivation, I am eternally grateful to both of them, and my other friend of the time, Catherine Jones, for what they said on my behalf because a bewilderingly short time later I found myself in London ready to start work at the Foreign and Commonwealth Office.

I was not only lucky to have got into the Foreign Office but also to start work there at a time when it was broadening its recruitment base to make its staff a better reflection of Britain as a whole. This initiative was later accelerated during Robin Cook's time as Foreign Secretary. It benefitted the Service and enhanced the job it does for the country by bringing in a wider range of life experiences, perspectives and skills to contribute to policy making.

It did my social life no harm either as it brought an influx of young people with similar outlooks from all over Britain to London at the same time. Our wages were modest but my friends and I left no penny unspent during a two and a half year tornado of pubs, clubs, gigs and parties. The experiences and scrapes we shared during that formative time created lifelong bonds that will never be broken.

As the saying goes, history never repeats itself but it does echo. Once again jobs are in short supply and the cost of living gap between London and the North of England, Scotland, Wales and Northern Ireland is growing. When coupled with the squeeze on public sector budgets, this means that the Foreign Office is in danger of falling back into recruiting only the well-off, privately educated and London-based. My hope is that this book, apart from being an entertaining read, might encourage a few more young, working class people from outside the South East to buck the trend and pursue such a career.

I cherish the twenty years I spent in the Diplomatic Service and recommend it wholeheartedly to anyone with an interest in the world and how it works. Having the opportunity to play a part in major international issues is well worth a few initial years of financial struggle in London. The Aston Martin never arrived and I drank more, much more, beer than Martini. But the exotic places, glamorous lifestyle and international intrigue I encountered make the Bond analogy a little less ludicrous than it seems.

2. London Town

I LEFT for London in May 1989 to embark on a life of high-flying glamour. However, my preconceptions took a blow when I first arrived in the capital. As was the norm for young, out-of-town recruits, the Foreign Office had found some initial accommodation for me in one of a chain of cheap hostels. Mine was located in Notting Hill, which was still an interesting area and had yet to transform from Rastafarian to trustafarian.

The hostel was a fleapit. When we arrived, my dad helped me through the door with my suitcase and promptly dashed straight out again to stop my mum coming in. The squalor would have given her a heart attack and I might have found myself being bundled back in the car home again before I had even got started. Apart from the filth and decay, I found myself billeted next to a ranting Post Office trainee with appallingly smelly feet and a window-rattling snore. More disturbingly, the place was home to numerous psychiatric patients, whose release into the community owed more to government cost-cutting than considered medical judgement.

The Accidental Diplomat

Fortunately, I was soon able to get myself transferred to a smarter one in Hampstead that was more in keeping with my exalted diplomatic status and the prevailing public health regulations. There were some good, fun people in there, including the less narcissistic of the National Youth Theatre students, a group of Irish nurses and a posse of Trinidadians. The latter two groups hit it off well together and introduced me to the surprisingly compatible pleasures of nearby Kilburn's Irish pubs and a carnival-esque approach to life.

It had its share of deranged residents too. The room-mate inflicted on me by the manager was an Alvin Stardust-lookalike motorcycle messenger, whose loudly expressed Christian beliefs were rendered unconvincing by his repulsive personal habits. Others were more entertaining, such as Martin, a large Geordie.

Aside from earning a lifetime ban from Pizza Hut for emptying the salad bar into a passing yuppie's convertible, he had a late night penchant for climbing - clad only in a pair of cowboy boots - on to the roof of the five storey building to blast golf balls around NW5. Overall, though, the Hampstead address attracted a less menacing class of the unhinged and was a decent place to stay for a few months until I was able to organise a house share with some colleagues.

More importantly, working at the Foreign Office was everything I had imagined and more. And I was hooked from day one when I struck lucky on the jobs front.

Most of my fellow inductees were allocated to the Finance Department, monitoring Embassy budgets and organising the pay roll. Foreign Office accounts are much like those of any other organisation and I would have found being sent to work on them a distinct disappointment. I was despatched instead to the Near East and North Africa Dept (NENAD), a thoroughbred that dealt with important Middle

East issues. This was dreamland for a foreign affairs obsessive like me. The ostensible content of my clerical support job may have been as prosaic as anything the Finance Department had to offer – filing, faxing and photocopying papers – but they were for the desk officers who analysed developments in their countries of responsibility and made policy recommendations to Ministers. The content of those security classified papers was endlessly fascinating.

In keeping with its status, NENAD was located in the magnificent old India Office, part of the historic Foreign Office building on Whitehall. My cramped room overlooked the marble splendour of the elaborately carved Durbar Court, an inner courtyard built in 1867 and inaugurated at a reception for the Sultan of Turkey. For a change of scenery, there were leather armchairs just down the corridor at the top of the red-carpeted staircase leading to the Foreign Secretary's office.

Such grandeur was a long way away from a hut on Hull Docks. As if to confirm the point, Princess Diana popped in for a visit one day during my early months there. Being a devout anti-monarchist, I ostentatiously carried on working rather than join the rubberneckers at the top of the staircase. Consequently, I had no idea when I charged round the corner on my way to the photocopier that the princess was coming the other way and clattered straight into her.

When I was not inadvertently assaulting members of the royal family, my first job in NENAD was to provide clerical assistance to the Libya and Jordan desk officers. Libya's crackpot dictator, Colonel Gadaffi, was the source of some laughs. He once gave a speech railing against the British theft of Arab culture, exemplified by the fact that the name of our supposed greatest ever playwright proved that he was actually an Arab – Sheikh Speare.

Overall, though, matters were deadly serious. It was hard to imagine in 1989 that the reconciliation between the UK and Gadaffi's Libya that took place a few years before his overthrow in 2011 would ever be possible. Our relations with them had been in the deep freeze since PC Yvonne Fletcher was shot dead from the windows of the Libyan Embassy in London in 1984, and a series of Libyan-backed terrorist atrocities across Europe. Colonel Gadaffi's regime was developing chemical weapons and we received reports on their progress. One consequence of this dangerous situation was that British companies wanting to sell any goods to Libya had to obtain an export licence from the UK government before doing so. I was put in charge of approving or denying their applications. Although I had a grade C 'O' Level in Chemistry and a working knowledge of where to put a hazardous chemicals sticker on the back of a lorry, this displayed an alarming degree of confidence in a newly-recruited nineteen year-old.

After several months, I was taken off Libya and moved across to work in NENAD's Arab/Israel Section, where the Jordan part of my brief was a more logical fit. It was an exciting time. The Middle East Peace Process was going through one of its more tumultuous phases and the first Palestinian 'Intifada' uprising against Israeli occupation was raging in the West Bank (which was part of Jordan between the 1948 and 1967 Arab-Israeli wars), Gaza Strip and Jerusalem.

Behind the scenes, the discussions were taking place that would lead to the 1991 Madrid Peace Conference, the 1994 Oslo Accords and Jordan's Peace Treaty with Israel. The Madrid Conference reinforced the principles of the 'two state solution' and an exchange of 'land for peace' that are still the most realistic basis for any solution to the dispute. There was a growing feeling that a peaceful resolution to this seemingly intractable conflict was within reach and it was enthralling to be involved, even in the most peripheral way. Sadly history proved us wrong and the Arab/Israel dispute is probably further away today from being resolved than it was then.

The high profile of the Arab/Israel dispute made the Section the focal point of the department. It also made it busy and I was given responsibility for drafting replies to Parliamentary Questions, MPs' letters and correspondence from members of the public. I am sure that at least some of the Honourable Members or my other regular correspondents, including the Chief Rabbi, Cat Stevens and the prolific Mr Jesus H. Christ of Hyde Park, Sheffield, would have been disconcerted to discover that their authoritative Foreign Office response originated from a teenager whose closest first-hand experience of the Middle East came from visiting a kebab shop in Camberwell.

Such delegation was one of the great pleasures of working in NENAD. The heavy demands on the experienced staff meant they had to pass, what seemed to them to be the more mundane tasks, down the chain. This gave me a huge advantage over my counterparts in quieter departments in terms of the experience I was able to acquire right at the beginning of my career.

Most of my senior colleagues were members of the Foreign Office's 'Fast Stream' – exceptionally talented officials who had been recruited from elite universities to be rushed through the promotion system. The majority had the intellect that entirely justified such special treatment. But one occasionally came across those whose academic prowess outstripped their real world nous.

A particular favourite was the recent Oxbridge PhD graduate who needed a delegation of four members of junior clerical staff to convince her that documents sent for faxing would be returned to her and did not need to be photocopied. We eventually realised that she was under the impression that the document went inside the machine and was squeezed down the wires before being excreted at the recipient's end.

That was very much the exception though, and the importance of the issues dealt with by NENAD meant that the people I first worked with, genuinely were amongst the Foreign Office's brightest and best. They elegantly made a demanding job look effortless and always seemed to have time to school a new young recruit, despite juggling multiple urgent issues simultaneously.

Perhaps the best of my desk officers was James Andrews, who combined great knowledge and experience with considerable charm and a well-developed sense of fun. James was well into his fifties but maintained a vigorously complicated personal life, which he used to offset with an annual trip on his Harley Davidson to a Trappist monastery in Scotland and a disconcerting habit of taking naps whilst sitting bolt upright at his desk. One of his pastimes was sneaking catchphrases from tabloid newspaper editorials into his erudite policy submissions to government ministers – the phrase, 'it is the only language they understand' featured regularly when he was recommending a firm course of action towards a foreign power.

I had a greater affinity for James's style than that sometimes adopted by the old-school tie brigade. It was a time of transition in the Foreign Office and some of the less appealing members of the old guard were prone to trying to preserve it as an exclusive club. They regularly, for example, used Latin phrases in their written work that were incomprehensible, and meant to be, to those of us from schools that left dead languages to rest in peace. Thankfully, such exclusionary penmanship practices were steadily stamped out by successive Foreign Secretaries, starting with, to his credit, the patrician Old Etonian, Douglas Hurd and the Service was better for it.

Aside from these linguistic nonsenses, I soon discovered that the Foreign Office was a lot less stuffy than I had anticipated and had a strong sense of camaraderie. One morning, soon after I had nervously taken over responsibility for the export licences, I arrived at my desk to find a note from one of my bosses asking me to call a 'Mr C. Lyon urgently about exporting fish to Libya'. The telephone number turned out to be for London Zoo. That sense of humour was very similar to the one that prevailed back in Hull.

Perhaps the biggest surprise was the culture of informality and the approachability of most senior officials. Everyone except Government Ministers, Ambassadors and the Permanent Under Secretary (the civil servant in charge of HM Diplomatic Service) was addressed by their first name, even by the lowliest members of staff, long before this became the norm in most workplaces. There was also an 'open door' policy, whereby you were expected to walk in to any office without knocking and only leave if another meeting was already going on inside.

After the C. Lyon affair, I was still not sure whether to believe that really was the established practice, especially when I was first sent to take some papers to our notoriously pugnacious Deputy Under Secretary – despite the double-understated title, this is a very important Foreign Office position, not a junior typist. But, as instructed, I barged into his grand, oak-panelled office and handed over the information without a hitch. Unfortunately, when I turned around to leave I discovered two identical, adjacent doors facing me and was unsure which of them I had entered by. Not wanting to look an idiot and being too shy to ask, I took a fifty-fifty chance, picked one and strode purposefully into his cupboard. 'Find what you were looking for, dear boy?' said the Under Secretary drolly without looking up from his reading matter, as I made my second attempt at exiting his office discretely.

The camaraderie was even more pronounced outside of work. I joined the Foreign Office as part of a large influx of young support staff from similar backgrounds in hard-living Scottish, Northern and Midlands towns and cities and quickly made a wide but tight circle of friends. We were all living away from home for the first time and sharing rooms in grotty hostels and flats that did not inspire early nights in.

The Diplomatic Service Football Club was the source of most of my closest friends. The team was mainly composed of recent arrivals in London like me, with a sprinkling of 'veterans' in their late twenties returning after a couple of postings overseas. Some of the lads had played for their city representative teams and had trials with professional clubs, so we were actually quite a useful team by Saturday afternoon park standards.

The trouble was that our ability was undermined by our chaotic organisation and lifestyles. The nadir came during my year in joint-charge of the team, when we led the league from the start and thought we had already won it before the last game of the season. Due to a missing goalkeeper and an excess of nonchalance, we lost that match 6-1. Unfazed, that Saturday night saw the mother of all victory parties. It was, then, somewhat deflating to discover on the Monday morning that the ride we had planned around London on an open-topped tourist bus would have to be cancelled. It turned out that I, abetted by a couple of fellow maths geniuses in the team, had added up the league points incorrectly and, by virtue of our shambolic performance on the last day, we had in fact missed out on the title on goal difference, by a single goal.

It was a measure of our unity that recriminations were minimal. We were a team in the best and most enduring sense of the word. The nature of Foreign Office life means that we are now scattered across the globe and though we do not see each other often, we all know that we can rely on each other when required. Even those of us who were the less talented footballers brought something important to the group; mostly a gift for comedy, a knack of finding house parties or, in the case of Steve Forsyth - Bacup's answer to Rick Astley - the ability to have the entire top deck of the number twelve bus rolling in the aisles with his renditions of popular song and dance routines.

London was not always the most welcoming place to a bunch of boisterous lads from all points north but we did not let that deter us from embarking on all manner of joyful, drink-fuelled adventures that I would not have missed for the world. Even when things went slightly awry, no long-term harm was ever done and we could always have a good laugh about it afterwards.

One such occasion came the day after a May Bank Holiday, end-of-season, trip to Brighton. I was quietly nursing a monstrous hangover in my office, filing at a glacial pace and trying not to hurt my head by rustling the papers, when the furious girlfriend of one of my mates burst in cursing me for getting her boyfriend arrested and demanding that I arrange his freedom.

I had no recollection of any such incident and began to panic about my memory loss being worse than I had thought. What had happened was that we had arrived in Brighton at 11am, having already had a few on the train down from London, and, fifteen hours later, had barely made it beyond the pubs and clubs within a hundred yard radius of the station. Some of us had ended up travelling back to the capital on a pre-dawn milk train. What I had forgotten was that our group had become hopelessly splintered in the carnage and one of the lads, Andy McKean, had been separated from his flatmates and keys. He was also missing his shirt and his shoes, for some inexplicable reason, as we had not got anywhere near the beach. As a result, Andy had come home with me to crash out for a few hours in the four-storey house I was sharing in Greenwich before going to work. In my addled rush to get to the office, I had completely forgotten that Andy was asleep on the couch in the basement until Louise, his girlfriend, had pointed this colourfully out to me in front of my bosses.

As he was also still being fuelled by something other than logic, Andy had woken up locked inside an empty house and decided that, rather than call me or someone else, the best course of action would be to borrow some of my clothes and exit via the kitchen window and back garden.

Unfortunately, it was a terraced house with high walls at the back and either end of the street. Finding himself trapped, Andy alighted on a neighbour hanging out her washing. She opted not to wait to see what the large, dishevelled Glaswegian wearing ill-fitting clothes and tumbling swearily over the garden fence towards her wanted and hot-footed it inside to call the police. Once we had confirmed his identity to the constabulary and he had been released, Andy was predictably magnanimous. Louise remained less than thrilled with both of us for some time afterwards.

The itinerant life of crashing out at one another's flats was a feature of most weekends and often the source of nearly as much entertainment as the actual nights out.

One Saturday morning after a typical Friday night before, I was half-woken from my comfortable resting place on the living room floor of some scuzzy flat in South London, which was being shared by my friend Alex Hill, by the sound of him dozily scuffling about in the kitchen. A short while later, Alex appeared at the living room door, fetchingly attired in vintage boxer shorts with several more holes than had originally been installed by C&A, with two slices of bread in his hand and asked if anyone had a lighter. Apparently the gas ignition for the grill was broke, as was pretty much everything else in the flat, including us. After receiving a negative chorus of unhelpful grunts from the occupants of the living room, Alex shuffled off again.

About half-an-hour later, I had roused myself all the way up into a sitting position and noted Alex, now, mercifully, fully clothed, showered and shaved, heading purposefully towards the kitchen with a box of matches in his hand. Seconds later there was a small roar and a jet of flame shot out across the hallway. This was followed moments afterwards by Alex shambling back into the living room doorway, this time with considerably less forearm hair, charred eyebrows and a lightly smouldering quiff.

Apparently he hadn't turned the gas off after his first aborted toast making attempt and it had been on the whole time he was in the bathroom. At that point, we decided to go to the caff for a fry-up instead and elected to keep our counsel when the other customers complained about the smell of burning.

At the time, London was plastered in posters for a long-forgotten, fire-based Hollywood blockbuster called

Backdraft. There did not really seem much point in going to see it after Alex's one man re-enactment.

In spite of my social life and occasional impromptu auditions for a part in a Whitehall farce, my staff appraisals during my two years in NENAD were excellent. That left me seemingly well-placed now that the time had come for the main business of Diplomatic Service life – securing a desirable posting overseas. First, though, there was another hiccup that almost stopped me from getting that far.

3. Our Man in the Basement

THE modern Foreign and Commonwealth Office (FCO) is a touchy-feely organisation that consults its staff and takes their circumstances into account before appointing them to overseas posts. But when I was awaiting my first posting in 1991, the 'mobility obligation' was sacrosanct.

It was a declaration agreeing for us to be sent wherever we were 'operationally required'. That was taken by Personnel Operations Department (POD) to mean with minimal possible effort on their part when it came to posting those of us in the lower ranks. Instead of painstakingly matching our CVs to the available jobs, they adopted the undeniably efficient management technique of pinning two old *Shoot!* magazine-style league ladders to their office wall.

One contained the names of junior staff, who rose up the chart as their turn for a cherished overseas posting came around. The other listed the posts that needed to be filled. The names of people and posts were then paired off simultaneously as they reached the top of the ladders. The random pairings this system produced did at least fulfill the Foreign Office's objective of encouraging its people to learn new things and become gifted generalists. Speak fluent

Swahili and have a flair for East African politics? Mongolia here you come!

There was one uncanny exception to this rule. In the case of the *Shoot!* ladder, it did not matter how low you placed Liverpool in August, because seemingly, they would always be at the top by May. In much the same fashion, whenever a Personnel Operations' staffer was due a posting, Kuala Lumpur would miraculously rise to the summit.

Things worked out slightly differently for my first posting. I had actually thoroughly enjoyed my time in London, despite acting like a stereotypical Northerner on a rugby league Wembley cup final trip by moaning constantly about the beer and the unfriendly locals for the best part of three years. But overseas postings were what joining the Foreign Office was all about and I could not wait to get away.

Waiting to find out where you are going next is the part of being a diplomat that fills the childhood void left by the loss of Father Christmas. I was an avid reader of all of the correspondence that came from our Embassies overseas and pretty much any other literature about the big exciting world that I could lay my hands on. As a result, I would have been thrilled with virtually any of the possibilities out there.

Sadly, the FCO had other plans. Instead of being left to take my chances on the league ladders, I received a surprise call from my Personnel Officer, asking if I would be interested in leaving London earlier than anticipated to do an Embassy administration job in Georgetown, the capital of Guyana, a small country on the South American mainland but one that is a former British colony and culturally Caribbean, rather than part of Latin America.

Apparently the offer was 'a reward for my impressive work in London'. The chance of getting out of the capital aside, I was underwhelmed by the proposal from the start.

Administration work was perceived as being higher up the career scale from the clerical support job I had anticipated being offered. But I hated all of that stuff – keeping accounts, ordering stationery and the like was really not my scene. It was the kind of job I could have found in companies closer to home and there did not seem much point in being in the Foreign Office to do it. In fact, I had been much happier filing papers and photocopying in the Arab/Israel Section in London because of the engagement it provided with an important global political issue.

I had no reason to doubt what I was told by various reliable sources about the Guyanese people being lovely and often incredibly beautiful, but the place sounded like the ultimate backwater in terms of foreign policy excitement. Worse still, it did not even have the other compensations I had imagined on first hearing about it.

Unlike most of the Caribbean it did not extend to palm-tree lined white sand beaches. Instead, for much of the year the place was a soggy swamp with a coastline like the banks of the River Humber, albeit with sugar refineries instead of petrol ones and considerably more mosquitos. The local political scene was dysfunctional and crime out of control. I liked Graham Greene novels but was not sure that I wanted to live in one.

Some of my older FCO football team-mates had already completed their first postings and returned to London. An informal chat with them revealed the reason for Personnel's unusual approach to finding a candidate. The lad I would be taking over from was a contemporary of theirs and notorious character called Davy Groves. He had achieved the rare distinction of being recalled from post in order to be fired from the Foreign Office. This was some going because getting sacked in those days was almost impossible. The normal sentence for offences up to and including sleeping with the Ambassador's wife, or failing to do so when instructed, was to be redeployed to the Stationery Department.

That happened to one alcoholic acquaintance of mine, who acquired the glorious job title of '3rd Secretary, FCO Christmas Cards' next to his name in the Office Directory. His sole function was, once a year, to send out packs of blank, official Christmas cards for use by our Embassies overseas, a modest task which still, sadly, proved to be beyond him.

It transpired that Davy's impressive range of misdemeanours included establishing a flourishing business selling officially supplied office and staff accommodation furniture on the local market to fund his exuberant social life. The mountain of other ignored tasks in his cupboard suggested that his rare appearances at work had mostly been to order new stock. The problem now was that Davy had gone AWOL.

Apart from the FCO's general reputational concerns about mislaying staff in the swamplands of the Americas, finding Davy was essential. His departure from post had to be confirmed and his diplomatic accreditation cancelled at the Guyanan Foreign Ministry before a successor could be despatched. This was proving tricky because the last confirmed sighting of him had been as he disappeared drunkenly over the horizon towards Barbados rowing a boat laden with soft furnishings from the Overseas Estates Department catalogue.

POD needed to line someone up to go out to Post at short notice once Davy had been retrieved. Aside from my misgivings about Georgetown, I had a more important reason for not wanting to go there. My much-loved grandfather was in the late stages of a terminal illness and I was not keen on going somewhere that was only marginally easier to get home from than Pluto. I decided that there was no choice but to turn the posting down.

I asked my line managers on how best to approach this delicate matter. Our Deputy Head of Department, Edward Milliner, was a nice man but not always the most hard-edged or practical. His response was to launch into a misty-eyed reverie about his long-held dream of sailing across Lake Titicaca and how a posting in Georgetown would allow me to live out this fantasy. In general, I shared Edward's romanticism about exotic foreign parts but, at twenty-one years old, all my fantasies had in common with Lake Titicaca was a couple of syllables.

My immediate boss, Nick Hood, was more pragmatic. Drawing deeply upon his expensive, classical education, Nick eloquently pointed out that: 'There is shit in every field, but more in some than others,' and advised me to decline the posting. His reasoning was that the mobility obligation did not apply because I had not actually been appointed but merely asked if I was interested in the job.

Bolstered by this advice, I rang my personnel officer and said a polite: 'Thanks, but no thanks'. After some desultory further efforts to extol the charms of the High Commission in Georgetown, my response seemed to have been accepted amicably.

I was still relieved at the ease with which this conversation had gone when I called Personnel again several weeks later to find out whether I had won the league ladder lottery yet. To my shock, the smooth response came back that I was no longer on the ladders because I had been lucky enough to be given a plum posting as Assistant Management Officer in Georgetown. My stunned protests were met first with a calm assurance that our previous conversations had never happened, followed by a more threatening: 'Well, we think it would be good for your career to go where we tell you'.

In addition to the actual reasons I had for not going to Guyana, stubborn Northern pride dictated that I could not accept being railroaded so brazenly, even at the cost of losing my Foreign Office career before it had really started. I told Personnel Operations that I was still not going and that it was up to them what to do next.

Fortunately, after a few weeks of pressure and prevarication, they decided that a punishment just short of sacking would be 'good for my career' and redeployed me to the Briefing Unit in Personnel Services Department (PSD). PSD was the unheralded ugly sister of Personnel Operations Department that looked after the administrative mechanics of moving Foreign Office people around the globe.

There was always a certain building hierarchy in the Foreign Office. The status of the Briefing Unit was indicated by its location in the basement of a small outpost in an obscure side street. It was far from the grandeur and buzz of the policy departments of the main office on Whitehall. My punishment was to fill stacks of briefing folders every day with the multitude of forms and information documents officers who were being posted overseas needed to prepare for their assignment. I think the idea was to make me contemplate the error of my ways as I performed this most menial of tasks. It would also compel me to notice, on a daily basis, how many of my colleagues were jetting off to foreign climes and that I could have been one of them had I not been so stubborn.

It didn't really work or, at least, not at first. For the most part, the only things I contemplated while stuffing the folders were the strangely attractive boxer's nose of Rebecca who worked alongside me and the whiff of ale from the pub courtyard our office backed on to. For someone who had come from a background of high unemployment in 1980s Hull, a few hours of mind-numbing work per day followed by several more hours of messing about, reading *Viz* and running the Foreign Office football team hardly amounted to breaking rocks in the hot sun. After the Georgetown fiasco, I was happy still to have a job at all.

The people in the Briefing Unit were great too. Most were the solid journeymen who keep the Foreign Office running but are not as career-obsessed as some of the keenest in the political policy-making departments. They were committed to doing a good job but kept this in proportion with having a balanced life. Nearly all of them had enjoyed, in the fullest sense, some interesting postings and I loved listening to their stories.

The Head of Section, Bob Book, for example, liked to reminisce about his days as the Consul in Fiji. It seemed that he essentially ran his office by walkie-talkie from a small fishing boat in the bay. About twice a month, his assistant would call him back to shore to deal with a lost passport or other minor emergency, just to give him a break from chasing marlin in the sunshine.

I was also located in the room where the post reports were stored. These were practical documents designed to provide all of the information about a prospective posting that an officer could need. I loved reading them because they gave an imagination-firing insight into life in all manner of unknown places.It is hard to understand now just how difficult such information was to come by in the pre-internet age and how precious these tiniest nuggets could seem. The merest details such as whether the electricity current in Ecuador was AC or DC and the options for skiing in South

Korea were enough to send me into hours of vivid daydreaming.

The authors of the reports on the most difficult places would strive to make them sound attractive to would-be job applicants. My favourites included the one on civil war-ravaged Beirut which spoke of the staff enjoying a, 'constrained but unorthodox and vibrant social life'. At the time, the social lives of several British citizens were constrained by them being chained to radiators in the Hizbollah-run basements of that fair city.

But we did get a hint of the vibrant side when a senior Embassy official called in to collect some form or other from us during a trip back from Beirut to London. Rumours of her estrangement from her husband appeared to be confirmed when she rolled in flanked by two strapping Lebanese bodyguards wearing matching fur coats and sunglasses; you can't be too careful when you are living on the edge, I suppose.

Rather than my time in Briefing Unit acting as a punishment, these glimpses of vicarious excitement from the outside world only stimulated my wish to get overseas as soon as possible. In hindsight, Personnel Operations Department may have been right all along because I was now bursting to go almost anywhere and do anything. After five months of folder stuffing, they chose to cash in on this by coming back to me with another proposal that nobody else was interested in. Only this time it really was an offer that I couldn't refuse.

4. Go East

EASTERN Europe was at the bottom of almost everyone's list of preferences for a posting. In my early years in the Foreign Office, during the death throes of communism, the region was widely dismissed as the preserve of masochists or those desperate to save money, as there was nothing to do or spend your wages on. Apparently there was room too for a dissident who had refused to do as he was told by the Personnel Operations Department. And, so, in the absence of a British Consulate at a salt mine in Siberia, I was posted to Bucharest, the capital of Romania.

The destination provoked pity from almost everybody I told about it. Romania was considered to be the worst of the worst of the ex-communist East. Unlike Hungary and Czechoslovakia, which began to open up in the latter years of the Cold War, Romania had been run in a hard line manner to the bitter end by Nicolae Ceauşescu. He combined the inadequacies of East European communism with the instincts of a megalomaniac dictator. This blend had enabled him to produce a purer form of sadistic oppression, economic failure and social catastrophe than had been achieved anywhere else in the region.

The Accidental Diplomat

Romania embodied the popular image of Eastern Europe as a dreary concrete wasteland suffocating in industrial pollution. The women were all reputed to be trainee shot-putters and the men piss-artists clad in stonewash denim with mullet hairstyles. The only apparent change in Bucharest since the fall of communism was the increased number of excursions by drunken miners to beat up students in the city centre. This was actually a tactic used by the government to deal with young protestors, rather than a popular leisure activity. But the overall impression remained disappointingly familiar to someone who had visited South Yorkshire in the 1980s.

Still, as there was no question of turning down two postings in a row and remaining in the Diplomatic Service, I resolved to make the most of Bucharest and do a good job in the hope that it would re-open the road to Buenos Aires the next time around. In any case, my own initial reaction upon being told that I was going to Romania was actually more intrigued than appalled.

At an age when many of my contemporaries were engrossed in Morrissey and Kenny Dalglish, my obsession was foreign news. I devoured books by foreign correspondents such as John Simpson as avidly as my friends read *New Musical Express* and was probably the only kid in the class who looked forward to *World in Action* as much as *Match of the Day*. Consequently, the idea of going to Bucharest soon gripped my imagination. It was mid-1991, and I was thrilled by the prospect of going to live in the place where the most tumultuous of Eastern Europe's revolutions had recently taken place, over Christmas 1989. My excitement was enhanced by an odd sense of familiarity with the key locations too because, contrary to the words of the great Gil Scott Heron, this revolution *had* been televised.

The 1989 Romanian revolution started in Timisoara when the feared and loathed Securitate secret police arrested a popular local priest, Laszlo Tokes. Timisoara is located in Transylvania - a clue in itself to how exciting Romania would prove, as no country of which Transylvania is a genuine part can possibly be dull - close to the Hungarian border. Illegally accessed Hungarian television made the city the first place where news of the collapse of communism elsewhere in Eastern Europe began to seep into Romania. This news emboldened a large group of Timisoarans to protest against the government. After a brief period of prevarication, the Ceauşescu regime started shooting demonstrators to encourage the crowd to go home.

A few days later, on 21st December, Ceauşescu called a huge rally in Bucharest to demonstrate that he was still in charge. In accordance with the established drill, about 100,000 people were bussed in from their workplaces and handed laudatory banners to wield, on pain of sacking or worse to anyone foolish enough to refuse. But rumours about what had happened in Timisoara had reached the capital and this time events turned out differently

In a staggering act of bravery, several people in the crowd began heckling Ceauşescu soon after he started his speech. The dumbfounded great leader had thought he was immune from the winds of change in Eastern Europe and made a failed attempt to stem the spread of dissent. He was quickly hustled away by his minders and hidden Securitate snipers began shooting into the protesting throng. The next twenty-four hours degenerated into pitched battles across Bucharest and other Romanian cities between the protestors and the Securitate. Differing units of the regular army initially pitched in on both sides before eventually joining the revolutionaries en masse.

The delusional Ceaușescu continued to believe that he was still adored by the majority of the population and refused to leave the capital. He made a fresh attempt to address the protestors the next day from the same Communist Party Central Committee Building balcony. Their hostility finally convinced Ceaușescu that he was in trouble and, as the crowd began to storm the building, he made a run for it.

The live Romanian TV coverage was cut when the rally started to get out of hand but restored in time to broadcast to an astonished nation images of Ceaușescu and his equally obnoxious wife, Elena, being half-carried by aides into a helicopter. The chopper just managed to take off from the roof as the first pursuers grabbed at the runners in an attempt to prevent it from getting airborne.

There then followed a demented chase across the Romanian countryside as the Ceaușescus were deserted one-by-one by their flunkies. After the helicopter pilot had faked an emergency landing and ran-off, the duo hijacked a car from a country doctor. They were eventually apprehended after coming to spluttering halt in a cloud of smoke near the town of Tirgoviste.

It was at this point that Ceaușescu may have experienced his first regrets about presiding over a system that churned out the Dacia as the only, scarcely, available car option. Unlike the cheap but decent vehicles marketed under that label today, the communist-era Dacia was an inferior local version of a failed 1970s Renault model and a wholly unreliable getaway car.

The next public sighting of the Ceaușescus was on Christmas Day 1989, when they were dragged out of an armoured car at a school in Tirgoviste. The school had been hastily requisitioned by the new National Salvation Front government in Bucharest as the venue for their trial. In the eyes of the desperate populace, the Ceauşescus had acquired the mythical status of indestructible vampires. The stated aim of the show trial was to prove that they had really gone from power. The token two-hour hearing succeeded in its objective by visibly reducing the Ceauşescus to the status of bewildered and irascible pensioners. They were then taken out into the playground and shot.

The trial was also intended to put an end to the battles raging around the country by encouraging the Securitate diehards still fighting for Ceauşescu to lay down their weapons. But it later became clear that the other communists who had exploited the mayhem to hijack the revolution and seize power had another reason for hurrying. They wanted to get rid of the Ceauşescus before they could reveal anyone else's role in their reign of terror.

In keeping with the chaotic circumstances, the execution was missed by the TV cameras that were supposed to broadcast the trial's happy ending to the nation over their Christmas meal. The firing squad were so keen to be the first to get their revenge in, that they were quicker on the trigger than the cameraman was on the record button.

Nonetheless, suitably grisly images of the slain dictatorial couple were transmitted around the country and to the rest of the world. That Christmas Day broadcast provided an indelible image of the Romanian revolution to fascinated foreigners like me.

Those unforgettable images were still imprinted in my mind when I set out for Romania in late 1991. We were banned by the Foreign Office from using their national carrier, Tarom, for safety and security reasons, so I took the only available alternative route on Austrian Airlines via Vienna. The already gleaming Vienna Airport seemed to have been given an extra polish just to emphasise that it was the last outpost of the glitzy West before descending into the dingy East.

Bucharest's Otopeni Airport could not have provided a greater contrast to Vienna and all it represented. In what was to become a familiar scene during my travels in Eastern Europe, the runway was lined with an aeronautical graveyard of decaying planes that had been parked there decades earlier and slowly dismembered for spare parts. We were then ferried to the terminal in a rusty bus that spluttered black smoke every time it braked to allow a lethargic pack of stray dogs to cross the weed-infested tarmac. Inside, the grimy windows and shortage of light-bulbs meant it was half-dark on a sunny autumn afternoon. Fortunately there were enough broken panes to allow some sunlight to stream in with the sparrows seeking crumbs from the grimy café tables.

Otopeni gave me my first acquaintance with the distinctive fragrance of early 'nineties Eastern Europe – an ever-present whiff of drains battling harsh disinfectant and mingling with the fumes of cheap cigarettes and low-grade, adulterated petrol. It may sound unappealing but I came to love the place so much that I eventually started to like the odour because of what it evoked.

After several months of excited preparation, including reading extensively, talking to anyone who knew anything about Romania and repeatedly viewing footage of the revolution, I was somewhat in awe of the brave people who had overthrown Ceauşescu by the time I got to Bucharest. This over-hyped immersion had left me primed to congratulate the first Romanians I met on their heroism. Perhaps fortuitously, my gushing excitement was quelled when the initial ones I encountered on Romanian soil were the border guards and customs officers. I was disorientated on first sight of them and momentarily thought I had landed in a dusty Mexican border town by mistake. They appeared to have been sent from central casting for a spaghetti western with their weary demeanour, two day stubble and ill-fitting uniforms that strained to cover their beer bellies. They reeked of anything but military discipline and derring-do.

The shambolic charm of Otopeni was to become a familiar pleasure over my time in Bucharest. One of my more enjoyable duties was to supervise the handover of the diplomatic bags every Wednesday afternoon. Such was the level of mistrust between the UK and Romania, these had to be taken in person to the plane by a member of the Embassy staff to make sure they were not interfered with by the Romanian security services. The smaller sacks of highly classified material were exchanged on the plane steps with a Queen's Messenger, who was sent out from London solely to accompany the bags in flight.

With luck, he would also hand you a precious selection of that morning's UK newspapers – there was no internet, mobile phones or CNN in those days, so we often knew little more about what was going on at home than if we had been on the moon. I would then settle down in the open back of the van to read the papers and sunbathe as the plane prepared to take off, using the diplomatic bag as a pillow for a couple of hours. Admittedly, this was more of a pleasure during the hot Bucharest summers than the sub-zero winters. The reverie would last until it was time to pop the main bag into the aircraft hold moments before it was closed and wait until the plane was airborne with the mail safely out of the clutches of the fiendish Securitate.

At my impressionable age, loitering in the sun reading the paper seemed an agreeable way to make a living and being given a pass to wander about on the tarmac of a foreign airport added a dose of excitement. Otopeni also offered its own desultory brand of entertainment to while away the hours.

First up were the baggage handlers, who had developed a system to make sense of the over-manning that was a legacy of communism. Rather than go right up to the plane, they would park the baggage truck about fifty yards away from the hold so that everyone could get involved in a game of toss the suitcase along a human chain. Some had safer hands than others, enabling me and Constantin, the Embassy driver, to engage in some excessively competitive betting on which handler would drop the most cases. Once this action was over, the ubiquitous stray dogs would wander over for a sniff of the West from the plane before giving their verdict by cocking their legs up on the wheels.

The potentially explosive finale to the show came when the plane was refuelled. This involved two blokes resembling Dr Frankenstein's dopey assistant Igor driving out in the most ancient, dilapidated fuel tanker imaginable. Igor #1 connected the tanker to the plane before retreating to the cab for a nap whilst Igor #2 held the decomposing, leaky hose up with one hand and chain-smoked with the other until the tank was full. Health and Safety was a liberal democratic concept that had yet to reach Romania.

I improvised my own measures by reversing our van twenty yards further away from Igor #2's Otopeni roulette routine of flicking his smouldering butts over the fuel puddles. Upon reflection, my precautions were a touch inadequate - a safe distance would have been somewhere in central Bulgaria rather than closer to the airport fence.

When I first arrived in Bucharest, I was installed in a sixth floor apartment in a centrally located block. It was there that my early weeks in Romania got off to a false start. During my pre-posting security training course I had my first inkling that Bucharest might not be quite as grim as predicted. I had expected the course to be a less than enthralling exercise in learning how to seal diplomatic bags properly and such like, which mostly turned out to be correct. But there was more to it than I had anticipated.

My job in Bucharest as a Registry and Communications Clerk would involve looking after classified files and operating a secure communications system between the Embassy and London. These responsibilities gave the registry clerks, in inverse proportion to their seniority, greater access than anybody in the Embassy to its state secrets and the means of communicating them. As our course instructor was keen to point out, this in turn meant that we would be of paramount interest to the notorious and still hostile Securitate.

After giving us a detailed briefing on the numerous le Carré type technical and psychological methods that the Securitate would use to harass us into submission, the instructor made an astonishing revelation that perked us up from our mid-afternoon sloth. Apparently, the Securitate had somehow got it into their wacky Bond-villain heads that a couple of young Registry lads barely out of their teens might be susceptible to free drink and the charms of the most beautiful female spies Romania had to offer. The free drinks from strangers in bars routine quickly lost its appeal, even to a Yorkshireman, when it was explained that they would be spiked with drugs that would cause us to blurt out every secret in our heads before collapsing in an unconscious heap.

The Mata Hari scheme was a different matter altogether. Our earnest instructor informed us that we must resist at all costs the temptation to invite into our flats the gorgeous, scantily-clad blondes who would inevitably knock on our doors demanding an English lesson. Apparently these highly-trained agents had no need to resort to dangerous truth drugs because they were able to elicit secrets, cypher codes and the keys to the kingdom from us by means of their sexual prowess alone.

And so it was that I spent my first month in Bucharest refusing all invitations to leave my flat outside of working hours. Sadly, though, the knock at the door never came and I was forced to accept that any adventure Bucharest had to offer would have to involve going outside.

Once I had got over this initial disappointment and reclusiveness, I went completely in the opposite direction and spent every spare minute exploring the city. For someone as fascinated by the Romanian revolution as I was, it was incredible to find myself living in the midst of such fresh history and walking around the places where these dramatic events had recently taken place on our TV screens. There were buildings at the top of my street that still had bullet holes in them and Revolution Square, with its burnt out University library and the Central Committee building from which Ceauşescu had been chased, were just a stroll away.

Even our Embassy estate bore witness to the physical impact of the revolution and the type of regime it had overthrown. Our Ambassador's former residence was located by the TV studios that were the subject of some of the most serious fighting for control of the country. It had been rendered uninhabitable by the battle damage it had sustained. The Ambassador was now housed in one of the luxurious former homes of Ceauşescu's most dissolute son, the alcoholic and alleged rapist, Nicu. Embassy lore had it that a routine pre-occupancy sweep of the building by our Security Department had found twenty-seven bugging devices in the toilet alone. That probably provides all the information anyone needs to know about why the Ceauşescu regime collapsed. As a general rule, any regime in which the President feels the need to bug his own son's toilet, and then has to install twenty-seven devices in order to get one of them to work, is doomed to failure.

Apart from the revolution sites, it was horrifying to see the scale of the damage wrought by Ceauşescu on the fabric of the city. In his later years in power, he had been gripped by full-blown megalomania. He destroyed vast swathes of historic central Bucharest to make way for his vision of a model capital. This concept bore more than a passing resemblance to the totalitarian dystopia portrayed in Fritz Lang's classic film *Metropolis*. As an indication of the level of madness involved, the building work included diverting an entire river underground and a failed attempt to wheel an ancient church to a new location on giant roller skates.

Size definitely mattered to the short-statured Ceauşescu and the avowedly straight central avenue of his new capital district was deliberately built to be more than double the width of the Champs Elysée in Paris. It was lined with flats intended for the party faithful and culminated in a vast square to accommodate rallies of hundreds of thousands to listen to his speeches from the balcony of the gobsmacking Casa Poporului (House of the People). In keeping with communist double-speak, the only people who were ever intended to get inside it were the Ceauşescu family.

This vast monument is the second largest single building in the world, after The Pentagon in Washington, DC. It is so big that it used up Romania's entire stock of marble and the design for its secret underground control centre incorporated a train system to get around it.

As was the case with most of Ceauşescu's grand projects, the Casa Poporului was not finished before his fall. This was partly because he was never satisfied with how it looked and kept insisting on changes to the design during his regular inspections of the site. Ceauşescu was right to be dissatisfied too. The building is hideous and somehow he managed to make such a massive structure look squat and dumpy.

The unfinished complex left a huge headache for the incoming authorities after the revolution. Some Embassy colleagues and I used our official contacts and a well-stuffed brown envelope to arrange an illicit tour of the palace with one of the Romanian officials charged with trying to work out what to do with it. He explained that it occupied such a large tract of Bucharest that simply knocking it down was not a realistic option, not least because its construction had cost the lives of numerous workers and a hefty chunk of the national budget. But completing it would require spending further fortunes that the country did not possess.

Then there was the issue of finding a practical use for an edifice on such a ludicrous scale. Our guide's problems became graphically apparent when standing inside the huge rooms. Ceauşescu's office, for example, was about the size of half a football pitch and the height of a two-storey building. Its enormity and the cold marble it was made from meant that the winter heating bill alone would be ruinous. It seemed appropriate to nick a broken piece of the marble floor, which has served as a handy paperweight ever since.

Despite Ceauşescu's prolonged assault on the physical fabric of the city, Bucharest still retained considerable charm. The ramshackle old Lipscanii quarter contained a terrific jumble of art, antiques and assorted junk shops. Contrasting refuges were provided by the semi-wild

Herestrau Park and manicured Cismigiu Gardens. And the streets of traditional Romanian houses, distinctively built sideways to the street, around the upper end of the long avenue of Calea Victoria, gave an insight into Bucharest's past as an elegant southern European capital.

For a modern history obsessive like me, though, the less cute but more vibrant newer areas of the city centre, such as Boulevard Magheru and its environs, held the greatest interest. This was where the place really felt like communist-era Eastern Europe, with its grey concrete blocks, retro-futurist architectural follies like the fake Intercontinental Hotel and clattering trams and trolleybuses.

At the risk of generalising unfairly, much the same could be said about the Romanian people. They too were damaged by the trauma of living under totalitarianism for decades but had somehow maintained a character and spirit that was impossible not to warm to. And, rather than in the more genteel parts of town, it was among the bootleg cassette peddlars and stalls hawking a cornucopia of scurrilous, but joyously liberated, newspapers and magazines that the best characters were to be found.

5. Off the Wall

IT was while on one of my first weekend explorations of the city that I discovered the Bucharest branch of the Michael Jackson fan club.

They brought downtown Bucharest traffic to a standstill every Saturday morning, moonwalking around the potholes the length of Boulevard Magheru. They then congregated on University Square to perform an enthusiastic re-creation of the werewolves dance number from the video to *Thriller*.

The club leader was a portly, middle-aged gent dressed in the best approximation of Michael's *Bad* outfit that Romania's scarce tailoring resources allowed. At the end of the routine, he would switch off the ghetto-blaster and pick up a megaphone to lead his followers in imploring the Swedish Committee to grant their hero the Nobel Peace Prize. It was not clear at first sight what had prompted this campaign or exactly how many biddable Committee members might realistically be passing University Square in Bucharest at ten o'clock on a Saturday morning. But you could not fault their commitment and entertainment value.

The Jacko fan club should be credited with finding a use for the empty plinth on which a massive statue of Lenin used to stand in front of Bucharest's main Soviet-style skyscraper. Although the culprits were never caught, it can only have been the fan club that surreptitiously installed a giant cut-out of Jackson adopting Lenin's classic hailing a taxi pose. The new incumbent quickly became a popular landmark and even the po-faced authorities were sufficiently impressed to leave it there for several months.

Of all the things that several hundred Romanians might have chosen to use their newfound freedom to protest about, campaigning for a Nobel Peace Prize for Jacko might initially seem an odd choice. But it made more sense after a little bit of thought. In the later years of Romanian communism, the ostensibly apolitical Michael Jackson was one of the few Western figures permitted to permeate the wall of censorship and propaganda. The ecstatic image of freedom and self-expression that he presented had given far more hope to the people now dancing on University Square than the words of any politician or human rights declaration. This was those people's way of saying thanks to the often maligned superstar.

I suspect the Jackson five hundred were also simply letting off steam. Romanians were subjected to an appalling array of pressures and pain under Ceauşescu. One of the most insidious was being kept in constant terror about who they could speak to and what they could say.

Romanians proudly boast that their language is the closest modern descendent of Latin. And, to generalise shamelessly, they have many of the warm and garrulous personality traits stereotypically attributed to Latin people. Unfortunately, people given to the voluble expression of multiple opinions and getting together in large boisterous groups are not the ideal subjects for a hard line, control-freak dictatorship. As a consequence, the Romanian communist regime enforced a particularly brutal form of social control. They let it be known that one-in-three of the population was working as an agent or informer for the Securitate. This was almost certainly a deliberate exaggeration.

But in a society where the government controlled access to all employment, accommodation and other public goods, the true number was still enough to inhibit even the most ebullient communicators. The regime went even further when it came to contact with foreigners – every citizen was obliged to report even the most cursory conversation with someone of a different nationality. This had the desired effect of ensuring that the few Romanians who had the chance to speak to foreigners mostly refrained from doing so. They were thus quarantined from any external suggestions that their rulers were not as marvellous as they cracked themselves up to be.

Carmen Bugan's 2012 memoir *Burying the Typewriter* provides a moving account of a dissident family's persecution by the State Police. The repression even extended to some of the Securitate's own people, as I discovered first-hand in the case of several Embassy colleagues.

All embassies employ a significant number of local nationals, especially in more service-orientated departments such as Administration and Consular – the section that processes passports and assists British citizens. They provide vital local knowledge, contacts and continuity to assist the diplomats who rotate in and out on three year postings. The vantage point this gives local staff inside the Embassy is sometimes exploited by hostile intelligence services.

In Bucharest, several members of the Embassy's locally-engaged staff were known to be working for the Securitate. Some were agents who had been placed in there of their own free will. Others, though, had been pressured into working for the regime by means of threats to their jobs, homes and families. Such fears were real because the brutal secret police operated with impunity and regularly carried out their threats, up to and including serious physical harm.

Such cases made me question my initial assumption that every Securitate operative was intrinsically venal and evil. Some of these colleagues were nice, seemingly ordinary people with whom one could socialise comfortably and, for example, be happy to have as teammates in our Embassy seven-a-side football team. Their stories made me wonder whether I would have acted any more heroically in their shoes. As one such colleague pointed out, people like him had felt condemned to do whatever it took to survive and support their families within a system that had seemed permanent.

This assessment that communism would endure was shared by the majority of Western experts almost right up until the moment when the Eastern Bloc collapsed. Whilst my colleague certainly did not deserve the admiration accorded to those who did resist, I found it hard to condemn completely someone who had faced dilemmas I had never been forced to contemplate. It was an early lesson in how foreign affairs work often involves shades of grey, rather than black and white.

Once the restrictions on free speech were demolished by the revolution, it was like a dam breaking. By the time I arrived in Romania, people had overcome any lingering doubts about whether it really was safe to say what you thought and even speak to foreigners. This was a fantastic development for a new arrival like me who was keen to learn about and get involved in the place. Being a foreigner still carried a certain novelty value and it seemed like everybody wanted to talk to me, sometimes all at once.

One person who talked to me way beyond the call of duty was my Romanian language teacher, Nadia Daciu. She was a human waterfall of entertaining opinions on everything under the sun. Nadia was the first of the remarkable, dissident-intelligentsia figures that I have often since had the privilege to meet in Eastern Europe. Despite being deprived of direct contact with anyone from the English-speaking world, she had taught herself perfect English by painstakingly, and illegally, listening to the BBC World Service and reading whatever literary classics she could lay her hands on.

It was also Nadia who inadvertently taught me how decades of intense propaganda can permeate even the most independent of minds.

In the course of our conversations, Nadia would regularly make scathing comments about the communist-style falsehoods she thought the new regime was perpetuating. She also often explained to me how she had protected herself against Ceauşescu's mind control by the simple expedient of assuming that whatever he said, the opposite must be true. Despite this healthy scepticism, after a couple of months of lessons something prompted Nadia to ask me: 'Where was it you said you were from in England again?' When I replied, 'Hull' she said excitedly: 'I thought so. We were cleaning out the wardrobe yesterday evening and it reminded me of how we used to collect shoes to send to you poor people.'

It was commonplace in Eastern Europe to portray Britain as a permanently 'foggy Albion' where the oppressed working masses lived in Dickensian conditions. Typically, the Ceauşescu regime had gone one step further in reinforcing the desired impression by conducting bogus second-hand shoe collections for the benefit of poor urchins like me. Of all things, it was this nugget that had slipped through Nadia's doughty defences against the bombardment of nonsense.

In addition to the sheer friendliness of the Romanian people, another extremely pleasant surprise for the new young man in town was the attractiveness of the women. Contrary to Western propaganda and the impressive record of East European athletes in the Olympic throwing events, very few Romanian women were built for the shot-putt. In fact, many of them were stunning – slender yet shapely, with dark hair, sharp, bright eyes and a slinky elegance to the way they moved and dressed. The dissonance between advance perception and reality meant that you could always spot a recently arrived foreign male. He would invariably have a black eye or bump on his forehead, caused by walking into a lamppost when he had found it impossible to keep his eyes on where he was going.

The general enthusiasm for meeting foreigners and, let's be honest, the disparity in affluence, gave the average Western man a glimpse of what life as a rock star might be like. Most were able to attract the attention of beautiful women they could previously only have dreamed about.

Unfortunately for us Embassy staff there was a frustrating and somewhat ironic hitch in this potentially heavenly situation. Whilst the Romanians had emphatically overturned all of their restrictions on contacts with us, the Foreign Office's Security Department still harboured the Mata Hari scenario.

Consequently, the Cold War era non-fraternisation rule had yet to be lifted and all intimate relationships with Romanians were forbidden. In fact, we were not even allowed to socialise solo with Romanians unless advance permission had been given by the Embassy's Post Security Officer. He was empowered to grant exceptions but only on the grounds that there were significant work-related benefits to justify it. Basically, an official dinner with the Prime Minister was fine but a drink with a potential supermodel, or even your next door neighbours, was not. This meant, in effect, that we representatives of the free world were now the only people in Romania living under the same restrictions that had appalled us when Ceauşescu applied them to the Romanians.

The rule seemed ridiculous, particularly to the single people in the Embassy, who had the greatest interest in it being lifted. My first objection was on the grounds of trust. If we could handle state secrets and highly sensitive material as part of our daily routine, then we probably also had the sense to realise what was not normal pillow talk. The second objection was that the very existence of the rule was what made blackmail possible. Banning something that regular human beings were going to do anyway opened the way to it, whereas allowing us to have normal relationships would have eliminated the risk.

My trenchant views on this and many other matters led to me becoming an informal shop steward for the junior staff. To the irritation of the more senior and securely married staff present, I raised the arguments against the non-fraternisation rule at every Post Security Committee meeting. In the interests of equality, I should state that this selfless human rights campaign had the full support of the single, female members of the British staff at the Embassy. This was noble of them because they were less impressed by the average Romanian male than us blokes were by the women, and only had eyes for the rugged technical works officers who came out from the UK to upgrade the Embassy building.

I would have advocated on behalf of homosexuals too but there were none in the Embassy then. In fact, officially, there were none in the whole of the Foreign Office. Homosexuality was a disciplinary offence that led to the removal of your security clearance, and, therefore, your job. The banning of it came as a surprise to me when I first joined. My still juvenile mind, fuelled by popular perception of the Foreign Office, had been more concerned that it might be compulsory.

Sadly, my selfless campaign did not succeed during my stint in Bucharest. Frustratingly, it was finally lifted a few months after my departure, when I was safely ensconced in the literal and metaphorical desert of Dubai. I did once opine on the phone to a friend in Bucharest that my former colleagues should give thanks and think of me every time some beauty was getting naked for them. But the ungrateful sod demurred, on the grounds that nothing could be more certain to kill the moment.

The supposed risk of serious disciplinary action did not stop some colleagues from fraternising, extensively, and a particular grievance was the selective enforcement of the rule when more senior members of staff were similarly involved. One was brazenly flouting it by living with a Romanian woman in his officially provided flat without any sanctions being taken against him. By way of compensation, this situation did at least provide the rest of us with a reliable source of comedy.

The gentleman in question was married and his wife had remained in the UK, apparently to see their kids through school there. But she was clearly suspicious because every few months she would jump unannounced onto a Friday afternoon flight to Bucharest to visit her errant husband. Luckily for him, his job meant that he had plenty of contacts at the airport and he always seemed to get wind of his spouse's arrival when she landed in Bucharest. As soon as the call came, he would turn pale, execute a Le Mans start out of the car park and race home. According to colleagues who happened to live in the same building and had in no way followed him back there to witness the show, the miscreant would then engage in a frenzied packing out of his mistress, her clothing and hygiene products, before pausing to smoke a cigar to kill the whiff of perfume. He would then return to work just in time to look pleasantly surprised when his visitor rolled up at the Embassy.

The non-fraternisation rule ultimately became unenforceable. The main advocate for its preservation, the staid Deputy Head of Mission and Post Security Officer, Charles Bingham, was not exactly the sort of older bloke who kept his finger on the pulse of what the young people were up to. He was blissfully unaware of how rapidly the social scene was changing and remained under the impression that the various, easy to monitor Embassy social clubs represented the full extent of it. Nothing could have been further from reality.

6. Cabaret Royale

IN the communist era and the immediate months after the revolution, there had indeed been few places to go out in Bucharest in the evening. As a result, most Western Embassies had a social club located in their dingy cellar that they extended to the staff of other friendly diplomatic missions and their resident citizens.

Each would open on a different night. For example, the Canadian Club opened on a Monday, the German Club on a Wednesday, the Brit on a Friday and so on. This restricted circuit meant the clientele could be repetitive, but these places were actually quite enjoyable for a while. Part of the reason was that the eccentricity of Bucharest tended to attract characters to match, such as the flamboyant resident Anglican vicar, Clive Thompson. He was followed around by a flock of strapping South Sudanese students and his party piece was winning bets by beating all-comers at darts, throwing underarm. This led to him attracting the unfortunate sobriquet for a man of the cloth of 'the underhand tosser'.

The German Club was the most welcoming of the venues, partly because their version of the manky cellar concept could be passed off as an authentic Bierkeller.

Shamefully, they also sold huge bottles of fantastic Hefe Weissen, a beer that was so strong it had even the most mild-mannered and diplomatic members of the British Embassy performing Spitfire impressions by the end of the evening. To the Germans' credit, they looked down on this sorry spectacle with pity, rather than offence.

Soon after my arrival the scene began to change. The first year after the revolution had been about stabilising a shattered country. But once that had at least been partly accomplished, enough people came into just enough money to go out and enjoy themselves. An explosion of new bars, restaurants and nightclubs followed to fulfil the demand. Due to the opaque licensing regulations, most of them were hidden away in courtyards, backstreets and parks, which helpfully added a prohibition-style frisson of illicit excitement.

Some of the early bars were a bit rudimentary. One enterprising soul a few streets away from my flat had simply installed some optics and a bottle fridge in his living room. The punters would just walk in through his open front door, serve themselves and park on the sofa. The landlord spent the evening sitting in his kitchen watching TV and only emerged to tot up what you had had when you were preparing to leave. Another place had gone to a bit more bother and created the basic air of a Wild West Saloon on the ground floor of a tower block – cowhide bar stools, wooden slatted doors and a Stetson on the wall. Their problem was that they had spent all of their start-up capital on the décor and not kept enough back to buy stock. On our first visit, all they had was a six-pack of Skol lager. Miraculously, scarcity made that godforsaken brew seem exclusive, as it could not be found anywhere else in Romania. The bar owners never revealed their suppliers but did give away their pricing structure somewhat by having twelve cans the next time we came in, then a full case of twenty-four the time after that.

Eventually, the bars started getting a bit more sophisticated and my favourite boozer opened up on the corner of Strada Jules Michelet, where the Embassy was located, and Boulevard Magheru, the main drag through the city centre. This unnamed place was all about location because of its unrivalled people-watching opportunities from their outdoor patio. In contrast to Bucharest's older establishments, it also broke the mould by not having a long, fantasy menu of unavailable items.

Instead, it restricted itself to an outstanding minimalist carte consisting entirely of fresh rotisserie chicken, chips and salad. And, to top it off, the bar featured the fun-packed prospect of Efes roulette. The barman blamed this involuntary, brain-scrambling game of chance on the disorderly stock-keeping system at the local Efes bottling plant. It led to different barrels of ostensibly the same beer having wildly varying alcohol contents. You would never know the strength of what you had had until you got up to leave. My embassy colleagues and I usually went there on a Friday afternoon after work. After admiring the passing, mini-skirted scenery for half-a-dozen rounds, people would start rising to go home and freshen up for an evening out. Most would manage the task with no ill effects. But every week at least one of us would collapse in a jelly-legged heap having copped for some rogue strong ones that had been left fermenting in the brewery for too long.

Most weeks the lucky Efes lottery winner would still manage to revive themselves in time to make it out later in the evening. Even for someone from Hull, a place that traditionally gets giddily excited about its Saturday night on the town, Bucharest's nightlife was too good to miss. The extra edge came from the fact that the experience was completely new to everybody present. There had not really been any clubs for young people there before and the constant opening of new ones, combined with the general sense of post-revolutionary optimism, created a near-euphoric atmosphere.

The music was tacky Europop – 'Rhythm is a Dancer' by Snap! looked set to become the new, post-communist national anthem at one point because everyone knew the words and it was guaranteed to get them on their feet. The surroundings were usually pretty basic too. But the punters full-throttle commitment to having the time of their lives, rather than posing or looking cool, was utterly infectious. It always felt like people were having both their first and last-ever nights out simultaneously and were determined to make it memorable.

One of the most bacchanalian venues was hidden in a park behind the Deputy Head of Mission's house. Late in the evening, as minds turned towards fraternisation, our smiles widened at the thought of him being unaware of what was going on just beyond the bottom of his garden.

But not even these joyous temples of pleasure could compare to the true pearl of early 1990s Bucharest nightlife: the cabaret clubs.

These venerable places had actually been around for years. They were the former haunts of both the pre-war and communist-era elite and a nod to Bucharest's slightly shop-soiled claim to be the 'Paris of the East'. That depiction might have been valid once but was now only visible through the bottom of a dodgy glass of Efes. The cabaret venues were mostly attached to grotty communist-era hotels and decorated in a style that might best be described as working mens' club on LSD meets flood damaged Moulin Rouge. For an insight into the off-kilter absurdity of Bucharest, the cabaret clubs were hard to beat.

All of them had their attractions but I had two favourites. The Spanish Club, had straw donkeys on the bar and sombreros on the walls. Inevitably the punters, scar-faced gangsters and callow diplomats alike, would end up wearing them by the end of the night. They also had low-hanging, brothel-red, draylon-tassled lampshades that served equally well when the sombreros ran out. Nor was it unknown for customers to wake up in bed the next morning to find a mutilated straw donkey staring back at them.

The star turn at the Spanish was a Romanian Tom Jones impersonator. Despite speaking no English whatsoever, he had mastered all of the lyrics of 'Green, Green Grass of Home' apart from the verses. These he would scat through pub singer style whilst gyrating his hips and incipient beer belly at warp speed. When he discovered that we were British like his hero, we quickly became firm friends, communicating entirely by means of the international language of the drunk and confused. I remember, loosely, staying up until dawn one night trying to teach him the words to 'It's Not Unusual'. I didn't actually know them when sober but fortunately the combination of Skol and Translyvanian red enabled me to dredge them up from some corner of my addled mind. Miraculously, the next Friday night, our hero aced it, especially the brassy 'da, da, de, da, da, da' bit. The sense of achievement brought tears to my eyes. Or maybe it was just the sharp metal lampshade fitting that was digging into my temple.

Good though the Spanish Club was, the London Palladium of the early 'nineties Bucharest cabaret club scene was the extraordinary Athenée Palace Hotel. The hotel occupied one side of Revolution Square and was a monument to faded glory or, more accurately, decaying ignominy. During the uprising, the Securitate snipers had taken a few rooms with unparalleled views for taking pot shots at the crowd. The façade was still heavily pock marked with bullet holes from the return of fire by the army. The Athenée Palace had been the epicentre of swinging Bucharest in the early twentieth century and Gestapo headquarters during World War II. During this heyday it had attracted every intelligence agent, dissolute journalist and sundry chancer within a five hundred mile radius.

In 1938, A. L. Easterman of the *Daily Express* called the hotel, 'the most notorious caravanserai in all Europe ... the meeting place of spies, political conspirators, adventurers, concession hunters, and financial manipulators,' while describing its 'ornate furnishings, marble and gold pillars, great glittering chandeliers, and the deep settees placed well back in the recesses of the lounge as if inviting conspiracy.' The *New York Times* foreign correspondent, C. L. Sulzberger, backed up Easterman's impressions in his memoir A Long Row of Candles. He described Bucharest in the run-up to World War II as, 'delightfully depraved' and the Athenée Palace as having, 'a corrupt staff always seeking to change a customer's money at black-market rates, and continual competition by ladies of easy or non-existent virtue to share the warmth of a client's bed.' Easterman and Sulzberger would have been happy to discover that their descriptions were equally valid in 1991.

By the time I first visited, there was no sign of the hotel having been renovated since the 1940s and its walls still dripped with intrigue and rising damp. I also had it on good authority that the practices introduced by the Communists lived on during the early post-revolution years, with the government bugging every room and tapping all the phones.

The managers were senior Romanian intelligence officers, the doormen did surveillance; the cleaners photographed any documents left in the guests' rooms and the prostitutes reported to the Securitate. All of which alternative activity may have explained why it was impossible to get someone to serve you a drink in the hotel bar in under half an hour.

The smoky and dimly-lit cabaret club in the basement was another matter. The drinks flowed fast and furiously in there. It was pricey too by local standards, with a round for six setting you back the best part of three quid. The female attractions at the bar were chatty in several languages and remarkably well-informed about politics and most other subjects, perhaps confirming that their employer was a more sophisticated organisation than the neighbourhood pimp. Then there was the entertainment, which ventured further into the surreal than anywhere else. At the other establishments, the topless dancing girls who came on between each act usually did a bog-standard can-can routine, which given their looks was still riveting. But the troupe at the Athenée would add a twist, such as coming on bound together at the hip by a gigantic, cuddly snake contraption. It looked like a pervert's production of *Sesame Street*.

One of the Athenée's star turns was a magician who shattered more illusions than a romantic weekend in Withernsea. This unintentional Tommy Cooper of the Balkans was as hopeless as he was hilarious. One evening's climactic showstopper came when he and his undeniably glamorous assistant locked themselves in a big black sack with a small bike lock. To fits of giggles from the packed house of fourteen people, they thrashed about for several minutes to no escapological effect. Eventually the drum-roll began to wane as the drummer's arms got tired and people began to drift off to the bar and toilets. When they returned some time later, they found the couple still locked in the sack and apparently motionless, prompting an anxious debate about whether the emergency services should be called. Finally, as dawn approached, the dynamic duo burst wearily out of the sack to a standing ovation and revealed that they had successfully swopped hats.

Whilst the cabaret clubs exemplified Romania's enduringly eccentric character, the rapidly expanding restaurant scene provided an insight into the changing nature of the country. Plush, new establishments, such as tennis legend Ilie Nastase's restaurant on the rear terrace of the National Theatre, were opening up every month. These places epitomised one of the perks of being in Bucharest - the easy access our diplomatic status allowed to the best establishments and their extreme affordability because of our hard currency salaries.

Nastase's served an ace steak and there was the advantage of being greeted by the great man himself before he adjourned to the bar to chat with the waitresses. The volleys of laughter that regularly erupted proved that he had lost none of his renowned charm and wit. His only fault was to be a shade chubbier than in his prime which meant his slick lounge lizard suit, and even slicker black hair, made him look like a descendent of Dracula. Suddenly being able to drop into such places for Sunday dinner after a couple of years of surviving on own-label fish finger sandwiches in London was a real eye-opener.

Whilst such luxury was great, it was the older restaurants that provided a glimpse of the times that Romania was steadily leaving behind. One of our favourite detoxes was to go to the Hotel Bucharest for a sauna and a meal. The Bucharest had previously been the exclusive preserve of Communist Party bigwigs from the Eastern Bloc.

It had a cavernous dining room and, as was always the case in such places in Romania, a menu to match. This vast, leather-bound document resembled a volume of the *Encyclopaedia Britannica* and listed every dish in the known universe. After a laborious process of elimination with the waiters, it would usually transpire that two items were actually available. These were frequently fried cheese or chicken livers to start, followed by some sort of chewy meat and greasy chips, which was actually better hangover food than it sounds.

The Hotel Bucharest restaurant's greatest attraction was its absurd over-manning and demarcation policy, which was a feature of the communist system that pledged to provide jobs for all. This quickly descended into parody. In one popular Romanian joke, Ceauşescu is showing the visiting Brezhnev around Romania's biggest tractor plant when the impressed Soviet leader askes: 'Blimey, Nicolae this is a huge factory – how many people work here?' To which Ceauşescu replies: 'About half of them'.

The hotel had turned the bogus ethos into a beautifully choreographed art form. My friends and I were frequently the only diners in room built for about four hundred. We used to run a weekly sweep on how many waiters would get involved in serving the meal but, despite the apparent dearth of work, they never stayed in one spot long enough for us to count them all precisely. After an extended period of trying to distract the nearest one from his intensive spoon polishing, he would eventually acknowledge your request for the menu. Two others would then carry it over, which was, to be fair, a double-hander job, given the size of it. Another would pop-up to take the order. Someone else would then saunter over to ask if you wanted a drink. A different bloke would put the beers on the table but amble off before taking the tops off. Then the bottle opener would step in. And so it went on, through at least two dozen different waiters until finally an old chap in a uniform you had not seen all evening would slip out from behind a pillar to pick up the tip.

Bucharest's only Chinese restaurant was located in the Athenée Palace and was equally idiosyncratic. It was a product of the great 1960s schism in the communist world, known as the Sino-Soviet split. That was when Chairman Mao's rebellion against Soviet hegemony created two rival communist camps and provoked several explosive skirmishes on the Chinese-Russian border. With an eye ever-focused on the main chance, Ceaușescu's crew had cosied up to the Chinese for a while and received various goodies as a result. The oriental restaurant was one lingering result of this obscure historical dalliance and had formed one half of a culinary exchange programme. I was never able to establish how well the fried cheese and boiled cabbage had gone down in Beijing but the Bucharest end of the deal was a real bonus. The food was passable and they often had as many as four or five of the eight hundred menu items available.

The staff at the Chinese place were masters of the cat and mouse game that characterised the city's old-style restaurants. A rather pleasant custom of Romanian hosts is to make sure that guests never have an empty glass until they expressly say no more, thank you. In restaurants, this meant that once you had placed your first drinks order, you would find that your glass kept being re-filled without any further requests being necessary. The older, cash-strapped establishments twisted this tradition into a handy revenue raiser. There you would find that as the meal drew towards its close, unordered drinks would start arriving at an increasing rate of knots. This would then culminate into an

It's a Knockout style frenzy as teams of waiters in outsized suits would scramble to slosh ever more drink into the overflowing receptacles on the table. The frenzy would continue throughout the inordinate period of time between the bill being requested and its arrival with the unwanted late additions included.

The game reached its entertaining peak one evening when our group was in danger of missing the kick-off at a football game due to the bill lagging behind the endless fresh bottles of beer and wine. A no-nonsense Glaswegian mate, John Weston, finally lost his rag at this fiasco. John had us in hysterics when he ended up sprinting through the kitchen and hotel lobby in pursuit of the head waiter, who was clutching our bill and kept throwing John dummies while his colleagues crammed ever more booze onto our table.

7. Democracy and Pork Bellies

A TESTING aspect of the heady Bucharest nightlife was that we registry staff had to arrive at work before everyone else each morning because no-one could get access until we'd unlocked the secure parts of the Embassy. Helpfully, the nightclubs would usually close just in time for us to get home, shower, change and head out to work. Even so, opening-up was a challenge because it involved disinterring a multitude of combination lock and alarm codes from your fuzzy brain and then opening them with shaky hands. But the knowledge that one false move would set-off a piercing din of sirens was a compelling incentive to get it right, even when in a delicate state.

The next task was to get the secure communications system up and running. The equipment was housed in an airlocked space hidden at the back of the Registry, a completely sealed room within a room that is raised up and has space all around it so that no bugging devices can penetrate it undetected. It is windowless and completely soundproofed to prevent any conversation within it being monitored from the outside. Opening the big metal door handle to enter the airlock felt a bit like going to work in a submarine. It was full of antiquated communications machinery. The machines were old-fashioned, heavy cast iron typewriters that belonged in a black and white war film. They worked by means of a complicated array of paper punch tape encryption ribbons that took hours of laborious typing to produce. Miles of this fragile tickertape spewed out of them all over the room and whenever some clumsy oaf, usually me about five minutes before home time, stepped on one of the ribbons and tore it, you had to start all over again. Such occurrences tested the capacity of the airlock's soundproofing.

The great benefit of the airlock was that, for security reasons, hardly anyone was allowed access to it and even the privileged few had to ring the bell on the front counter first. That made it an excellent place to hide after a heavy night. It was improved further as a sanctuary when a camp bed was provided during a Foreign Secretary's visit so that I could spend the night in the Embassy to receive any urgent messages from London. Nobody ever asked for the bed back, we kept forgetting to mention it and eventually hid it in there.

The man who spent the most time crashed out on the camp bed was Danny Wilson.

Danny was a smashing lad and one of the few people who did not have to compromise his staple diet when he was posted to Bucharest. As he had done in the UK, he lived on baked beans, boil in the bag curry and Boddingtons Bitter, all of which could be ordered in bulk on the monthly mail order delivery truck.

Sadly, such dietary habits did not make him the ideal man to share an airlock room with. Some olfactory relief was at least provided by his chain-smoking. Danny had been a steady smoker in the UK. But when he discovered that a box of 200 Marlboros cost considerably less in Romania than a pack of 20 at home, he upgraded to a fag-a-minute habit based on the faultless logic that the more you smoked the more you saved.

Apart from communications, the other main duty in the Registry was maintaining the classified files. Ostensibly this was a dull, repetitive task of cross-referencing every document in two registers and placing them on file. But I actually rather enjoyed it. Apart from gratifying my mania for order, it allowed me to take advantage of the registrar's position of being one of the few people with an overview of everything that was going on in the Embassy. It was a fascinating time. One part of the Embassy, the 'Know How Fund', was doing everything possible to help Romania to develop its nascent democratic institutions. Meanwhile, the Political Section was uncovering information that the revolution had been hijacked by former communists who were less set on reform than they would have people believe.

For reasons of public health and personal preference, we settled into a routine whereby Danny did most of the communications work and I did the filing. He was quite happy handling the cantankerous machinery from the comfort of his camp bed and keeping him locked away in the back room allowed me to present an image of efficiency on the front desk.

In the course of my filing duties, I found some old ones from the 1970s and 80s that should have been destroyed when the Embassy was evacuated during the revolution. One of them covered the Ceauşescus state visit to the UK in 1978. At the time, he was showing signs of independence from the Soviet Union and had withdrawn from the Warsaw Pact. Our invitation was an attempt to capitalise on his vanity and to sow further division in the Eastern Bloc. The visit was now, of course, an embarrassment for the UK. On the eve of Ceauşescu's execution, the Order of the Bath that he had been awarded during the trip was withdrawn as a gesture of atonement.

According to Embassy folklore, the visit had not gone well behind the scenes. The Ceauşescus had several of the psychological disorders that are common to dictators and had allegedly made no attempt to rein them in for the Queen's benefit. Amongst other offences, Nicolae was said to have ostentatiously wiped his hands with disinfectant alcohol immediately after shaking hands with Her Majesty and to have stolen the gold taps from one of the palace bathrooms. Presumably the poor man had understood the Order of the Bath to mean that he could dismantle it and take it with him.

Back in the new era, political excitement reached a fever pitch in early 1992 when the first free Romanian elections were held. In the weeks running up to the vote, Bucharest city centre saw a series of the biggest and most fervent political rallies since the revolution. There was also plenty of tension. At one I attended, there had been a double booking on Revolution Square by the main centre-left party and a nasty, far-right outfit led, bizarrely, by Ceauşescu's former court poet, Corneliu Vadim Tudor. Fortunately there were only a few minor scuffles as the fascists, not uncharacteristically, limited themselves to throwing the odd insult from a safe distance beyond the substantial riot police cordon.

On the weekend of the election, the Embassy dispatched its staff around the country to act as observers. We were licensed by the election organising committee to descend on any polling station anywhere to verify that the process was free and fair. Our main role was to ensure that no-one was adhering to the old Eastern European maxim, recently seemingly revived in Russia by President Putin, of 'vote early, vote often'.

I went with a couple of visiting election officials from the UK and one of our Defence Attachés, Bob Harris, to Piteşti and the surrounding region of Argeş County. Bob was a good partner to get as he was experienced in wandering unobtrusively around strange places looking for malfeasance. In Romania, he spent much of his time traversing the countryside dressed as a birdwatcher, deploying his binoculars and camera in search of those rare species that liked to nest near military airfields.

Piteşti is a medium-sized town in the centre of Romania. Like most it was pleasantly laid-out with a few remnants of the unique and attractive traditional architecture. But most of it had been subsumed by the communists' soulless concrete fetish. The East and West had rival visions of the future during the peak years of the Cold War. The West was convinced that tin foil would be the main manufacturing material of the 21st century and that jet packs would be the dominant transport system. The more grounded Easterners put their faith in cheap concrete and Dacias. A stroll around Piteşti showed how the East had got considerably closer to turning its vision into reality before the dream ended in 1989. To be fair to Ceauşescu and his predecessors (although goodness knows why we should be) they had had some assistance with the demolition work in Piteşti. It was the home town of Romania's 'Iron Guard' Nazi puppet leader, Ion Antonescu, during World War II. It was also one of the most industrialised areas in the country, playing host to numerous factories and oil industry installations. Consequently it had also been extensively remodelled by the allied air forces.

We arrived at the decaying former Communist Party-run hotel in the centre of the city on the Friday evening before the elections on the Sunday. It had all of the standard amenities of such establishments at the time – torn carpets, plentiful mould, sporadic water the colour of HP sauce and electricity sockets hanging out of the walls. There were no other customers.

Our first task was to find some dinner. Previous experience of similar hotel restaurants compelled us to take a walk around the town in search of an alternative. The scarcities that were a feature of the difficult transition from communism were often most evident when performing everyday activities and the problems were more pronounced outside of the capital.

Even in Bucharest, supermarkets were non-existent and all food shopping was done in outdoor markets and small grocery stores. Romania is a fertile country but the food supply chain had been wrecked by Ceauşescu's agricultural policy. Searching for meat was a forlorn task as there were frequently only a few scrag-ends of some indeterminate beast available. Fruit and vegetables were a bit more accessible in season although the lack of pesticides meant that half of whatever you bought would be worm-ridden. In winter, the markets presented a pitiful scene, with the poor farmers perched on the kerbside trying to make a living from the handful of rotten carrots or potatoes they had to sell.

The only foodstuff that was consistently available was eggs. The problem with them was transportation. Sometimes there was a shortage of the most mundane things in Romania and one such item was egg boxes. That meant the market traders had to fill the boot of their dilapidated cars with piles of loose eggs and bounce for a hundred kilometres along pot-holed roads from their farms to the markets in town. They would then sell them straight out the back. It was always a source of wonder to me how few they managed to smash because, whenever I bought half-a-dozen, I would ruin their efforts by breaking at least three in my carrier bag on the short walk home.

The shortages meant that new arrivals quickly grasped the Eastern Bloc shopping mentality of always carrying a plastic bag around with you, whether you were out shopping or not. It enabled you to buy as much as possible of any potentially useful item you stumbled across before supplies ran out again. Any surplus could always be passed on to grateful friends, who would return the favour when they struck lucky. But some apparent consumer oases turned out to be mirages. I remember once running excitedly across a busy road clutching my trusty plastic bag because I had spotted a usually empty grocer's window that was overflowing with new products. When I got there, the shop was indeed stocked to the ceiling but unfortunately with only one item – thousands of rough toilet rolls that appeared to have been shaved directly off trees, with visible splinters that brought tears to the eyes just from looking at them.

Piteşti was a textbook example of Romania's food supply problems and even eagle-eyed Bob could not spot any alternatives to the hotel restaurant. Our doubts about what, if anything, might be actually available there led us to ignore the extensive menu and ask the waiter what the night's 'special' was. My fingers were crossed, more in hope than expectation, that they would at least have some Caşcaval Pane (fried cheese in batter). I was already wondering whether I had brought enough Rich Tea biscuits from the Embassy shop to survive until Monday when, to our surprise and delight, the waiter recommended pork chop, egg and chips. Even more surprisingly it wasn't bad and we came down for breakfast the next morning with more hope than dysentery in our bellies.

The unorthodox but very edible 'breakfast special'

turned out to be pork steaks, egg and chips. And so it continued, through pork ribs, leg of pork, belly of pork and, on the final morning, some coarse pork sausages. We feasted on pork for three meals a day over the next three days. There seemed no need to offend anyone's pride by asking directly what lay behind the limited yet tasty menu but clearly a hospitable hotel staff member had acquired a pig to feed to the foreign guests.

On election day, we split up and fanned out around the region. I found myself travelling through the nodding donkey wells of the dilapidated oilfields deep into rural territory. You did not have to travel far into the suburbs of Romania before horses and carts became the primary mode of transport. In fact, it was pretty common to find them trundling along the fast lane of an unlit duel carriageway after dark, invariably transporting logs or scaffolding poles that were twice as long as the cart. They were illuminated only by a grubby rag tied to the end of the longest protuberance, which kept you on your toes when driving at night. In rural Argeş County, these horses and carts were the only visible form of transport crawling down the rough tracks to the villages.

I was warmly received everywhere I went and people seemed genuinely grateful for our interest in supporting their new democracy. Throughout the day, I witnessed nothing untoward at any of the polling stations I visited. The process was well-organised and all I noted was the inspiring sight of people queueing excitedly but patiently to exercise their hard-won democratic rights. But this dull run of worthiness came to a sharp halt at the final polling station I called on before returning to Piteşti to observe the count.

As we drove up a narrow, dusty lane, I could see and hear all hell breaking loose outside the small wooden local council building that was serving as the polling station. I got out of the car to find a small, bespectacled middle-aged man in a pork-pie hat trying desperately to hold the door closed against a crowd of about 60 head-scarved ladies of a certain age. They were yelling and pushing in fury. Then there was a sudden eclipse and the daylight faded in the narrow side-street. I looked up to see the largest man I had ever seen in my life striding towards us in his Sunday best battered tweed jacket and a formerly white vest. It looked like things were about to get messy and I began to beat a hasty retreat to the car.

But, rather than knocking heads together or slinging the most raucous protestors over his shoulder, he proceeded to greet me cheerily before deftly bringing order to the chaos by gently scolding the electoral officials and sweet-talking the irate blue-rinse mob into an orderly queue. No doubt being seven feet tall and twenty-odd stone helps in getting a hearing but, even so, this was an impressive performance.

Once his work was done, he came over to introduce himself and apologised politely for the conduct of his fellow villagers. Inevitably, he went by the name of Little Nicky and introduced himself as the local mayor's assistant. I expressed admiration for his efforts and asked him what on earth the trouble had all been about. 'Well,' he said, 'These ladies have been working in the fields all afternoon and then had to get dinner ready for their families, so this is only time they could come to vote. But the problem is that *Dallas* is on in fifteen minutes and they were worried they were going to miss the start'.

And you could understand the poor ladies dilemma. After twenty years of nothing but Ceaușescu in power and TV pictures of him occasionally visiting their oil derricks, how on earth were you supposed to choose between voting and the adventures of JR Ewing?

8. Bananas are not the Only Fruit

I WAS never a TV soap opera fan but the radio was a catalyst for my lifelong fascination with all things foreign. I spent many childhood evenings huddled under the covers at bedtime listening to commentaries of matches played by British football teams in exotic corners of Europe. In those pre-internet, pre-wall-to-wall coverage days, nowhere seemed more adventurously alien than the lands behind the Iron Curtain.

One outstanding memory was the 1984 European Cup semi final between Liverpool and Dinamo Bucharest. The tone was set in the first leg at Anfield, when Dinamo's captain, Lica Movila, engaged Graeme Souness in a debate that ended with his jaw leaving Merseyside in more pieces than it had arrived. The incident enraged the Romanians, who spent the next two weeks working themselves up into a frenzy of intimidation to be directed at Liverpool for the second leg in Bucharest. Unfortunately for Liverpool, most major Eastern Bloc clubs were tied to an organ of the state. Dinamo were particularly well-placed to make life unpleasant for their visitors because they belonged to the notorious Securitate.

The Accidental Diplomat

The return fixture was one of those rare games that did feature on live TV and Dinamo's backers had excelled themselves in assembling a hostile crowd of 60,000 in the 23rd August National Stadium, composed mainly, it seemed, of uniformed security men. Liverpool rose emphatically to the challenge and won the game 2-1. The abiding memory was of Souness strutting off the field at the end with his socks and legs in bloody tatters, having given a midfield masterclass in the midst of a continuous assault. His performance was still being talked about with awed respect by Romanian football fans when I arrived in Bucharest seven years later and a chance encounter in the centre of the capital soon gave me the opportunity to visit the scene of his triumph.

I was initially in no rush to go to a Dinamo game because their unsavoury connections meant there was no chance of me adopting them. My assumption was that I would end-up following their best-known local rivals, the 1986 European Champions, Steaua Bucharest, instead. Indeed, I did end up attending many of their games. But the club I really fell for in Romania was one I had barely heard of when I first arrived in the country.

The deal was sealed during one of my Sunday afternoon strolls through the city centre. There I came across a group of about a thousand people joyously banging ancient drums, blowing ratty plastic horns and generally creating an almighty breach of the peace. Some of them were shirtless - due to not actually having a shirt to wear that day, not posturing macho stupidity. A few others were even shoeless and had clearly spent the household clothing budget on gold teeth instead. Most had the deep bronze skin that comes from laying tarmac in the sun for years. Intrigued, I tagged along for a while and discovered that these were fans of the capital's less garlanded club, Rapid Bucharest. They were trying to save the tram fare by walking about ten miles across the city to a derby game against the despicable Dinamo.

I chickened out of completing the march all the way with them but made sure I got down to the National Stadium later that evening. Rapid's fans outnumbered those of the more heralded home team by at least three to one. They were terrific, backing their team with a heart and intensity that you only get from tight working-class communities, where the club is an intrinsic part of the people's identity. The mixture of coarseness and delirium was oddly reminiscent of rugby league at the Boulevard, the old home of my beloved Hull FC.

The game itself was an entertainingly spiteful affair. Dinamo were cynicism personified. Rapid lost patience with Dinamo's devious antics and proceeded to kick honest, straightforward lumps out of them. The climax came when the Rapid captain made a bid for immortality and poleaxed his infuriating opposite number with a right hook. The man who had been, de facto, refereeing the game was left unconscious on a stretcher while the actual man in black gave the Rapid skipper his marching orders. He was given a standing ovation all the way to his early bath.

My suspicions about the reasons for this fury and loathing of Dinamo came into sharper focus when I attended my first Rapid home game the following weekend. Outside the main entrance was a small memorial to the members of the Rapid club who had been killed in the 1989 revolution.

In fact, the animosity went further back than the revolution. For decades, Dinamo and Steaua had exploited their status as clubs run by the state security apparatus to dominate the league. One of the duo's dubious practices was to purloin promising young players from other clubs by drafting them into the army (Steaua) or the police (Dinamo).

Another was to advise referees and opponents that letting the pet clubs of a vicious dictatorship win would be good for their job prospects, home lives and, not least, anatomies.

For all that they had plenty of reasons to be bitter, Rapid's fans wore this history lightly.

More than anything, they were excited about the restoration of a level playing field after the revolution. They were proud to have merely survived the Ceauşescsu era and somehow maintained their status as the best supported club. They had done so partly by amplifying their links to the railway workers union and its deep roots in the resolutely working class district of Giulesti. This made it awkward for rulers who wanted to maintain a pretence of being pro-worker to shut them down. Instead, the regime contented itself with making sure that Rapid were never in a position to challenge its flagship clubs or repeat their 1966/67 title success. On that occasion their hardy supporters had hiked the sixty-odd miles to Ploiesti for the decisive final game – about 250,000 of them, if you believed all of the people who wanted to tell you about it by 1992.

In the post-revolution era, Rapid's anti-establishment credentials meant there was a certain cachet attached to following them. This led to the ridiculous spectacle of former communist apparatchiks turned democratic politicians pitching up at games pretending to have been lifelong fans. There was nothing chic about the Giulesti stadium experience though. The ground was a three-sided horse-shoe because the rebuilding work on one end had ceased years earlier and it had been declared unsafe. That was rendered comical when you ventured into the so-called safe parts. The dilapidated structure was seemingly made entirely of wood but, fortunately, the amount of beer and urine that had been spilt on it over the years mitigated the fire hazard, although the degree of rot was terrifying. To add exhilaration to the terror, Rapid's fans were in the habit of jumping up and down in unison, which made the whole thing shake like a bouncy castle. Giulesti remains the only stadium I have ever been in that forced you to take part in a Mexican wave even when you were sitting still.

The fans had a great sense of fun too. One match, the first after the mid-season winter break, saw possibly the biggest snowball fight in history rolling continuously around all three sides of the ground. Once the hooch, Tsuica – Romanian plum brandy - kicked-in, the scene began to resemble a Wild-West Saloon brawl, with victims tumbling backwards down the terraces into the chicken wire perimeter fence, as the combatants parted like the Red Sea to let them pass. Meanwhile, in the half-forgotten game on the pitch, the players and officials eventually tired of being caught in the crossfire and agreed to let corners be taken from a good five metres in from the flag.

Nor were Rapid fans any great respecters of authority. During my first year in Bucharest, I arranged to hire Rapid's indoor sports hall behind the ground for our regular five-a-side games against other Embassies. This led to me becoming friendly with the lovely people who ran the club and being presented with two season passes for the directors' box. Even that had no permanent seats, so it offered sitting on a very comfortable dining room chair with the plastic covering from the shop still on. They were brought out from the boardroom and placed under the only bit of corrugated plastic roofing in the whole stadium.

At my first game following their generosity, I was revelling in my new elite status when the rain started coming down torrentially. Any smugness about being amongst the only dry people in the house came to an abrupt end when the box was invaded by what felt like thousands of fans seeking shelter from the elements.

Giulesti is a district with a large Roma community and I spent my first game as a Rapid VIP with a large, scantily clad Romany gentleman perched on each knee. This turned out to be great fun as they shared their Tsuica, sunflower seeds and voluble opinions about the game although it was evident that the running water for bathing had been off for several weeks in the area. The man whose turn it was that week to be Prime Minister in the unstable Romanian government was seated two chairs along from me and rather less amused. His quest for the common touch had clearly led to him receiving more of it than he had anticipated.

The only footballing pleasure I craved that Rapid were not yet in a position to provide was first-hand experience of the European and international competitions I was enthralled by as a youngster. That required a trip to Ghencea Stadium, the home of Steaua, who were still a formidable outfit in the early 1990s. The remnants of state support remained in place and the playing squad had not yet been asset-stripped by richer Western clubs. Their potency at home, especially in European competitions, was considerably enhanced by the daunting experience foreign teams had to go through when they came to visit.

It is easy to forget nowadays just how alien and downright sinister places like Romania seemed twenty years ago. Once sides playing at Steaua had left their crumbling, grey concrete hotel, the first test they had to negotiate was the journey to the ground. The main route from the city centre was down the long, cobbled and severely potholed Boulevard Ghencea. The streetlights rarely worked, so it was pitch dark, with only the coach's headlights to illuminate the mysterious smoke and floating plastic filaments that drifted in the air. All along the road, the team bus would be surrounded by ferocious chanting from the gloom by unseen hordes of Steaua fans heading to the match, who would bang on the windows as it crawled along.

Having survived the ride to the ground, the visiting players would then have their nerves further jangled on arrival. As Steaua were the army club, their stadium was in a part of town almost entirely occupied by military bases and personnel. There was always an air of conflict about East/West sporting encounters during the Cold War. The omnipresent soldiers and Eastern Bloc military hardware around the ground ensured that the perception lingered on for years afterwards.

Ghencea stadium itself was actually borderline plush by the local standards of the time in that it had individual plastic seats rather than rotten wooden benches. The only problem was that the low grade plastic used meant that they had an alarming tendency to burst into flames when they came into contact with cheap fireworks, as they frequently did at Steaua. None of this luxury was apparent to the visiting team when, by now feeling rather a long way away from home, they emerged to face a screaming, whistling wall of noise from the stands packed tightly around the pitch.

My first experience of Ghencea actually came in a somewhat sanitised form when Wales were in town to play Romania in a qualifying game for the 1994 World Cup finals. Our Ambassador was more of an opera man and had eagerly passed on his complimentary pair of VIP tickets to a couple of more appreciative British Embassy representatives. Showing an impressive early grasp of the freeloading skills that are the hallmark of the junior diplomat abroad, my colleague and I arrived at the ground several hours before kick-off for the hospitality in the VIP room under the main stand. Our timeliness was rewarded with an impressive array of Transylvanian plonk and all the pickled vegetables a young man could eat. Once we too were nicely pickled, we ducked and dived our way under the preposterously large General's hats sported by everyone else in the room and made our way to our seats.

Even through the medium wave static and muffle of the bed covers, it had been apparent from my childhood radio days that Romanian football crowds made a bit of a racket. I had already had a live taste of this at Rapid but nothing could have prepared me for the sheer thrill of that international atmosphere for the first time and the noise that exploded when the teams came out. Sadly for Wales, nothing had prepared them for it either. They had already looked winsome in the warm-up, despite boasting top players such as Ian Rush and Neville Southall and noted hardmen like Kevin Ratcliffe and Mark Hughes. Once the game started, they were blown away by the crowd and a stunning Romanian performance orchestrated by the great Gheorghe Hagi at his peak.

Hagi had inevitably been one of the first Romanian players to leave the country after the revolution had opened up the freedom to do so without government permission. Now his every return from Real Madrid to play for Romania was treated as a triumphant homecoming. On this occasion, he did one of the most remarkable things I have ever seen on a football field. Having received the ball near the touchline about forty yards from goal, Hagi turned to the crowd and motioned to them as if to ask, 'shall I hit it?' The answer roared back in the affirmative and Hagi duly unleashed a rocket that flew over the head of Southall and into the net.

Romania were four goals up at half-time and went into Harlem Globetrotters mode for the second half, barely giving Wales a touch of the ball and pulling out all manner of party pieces. At one point, they recreated the playground classic of playing a one-two around Southall in his six-yard box, only to spoil it by getting muddled over who was supposed to get down on all fours on the goal-line to steer the ball in with their arse.

Infuriatingly, this rampant confidence often disintegrated when the team went overseas, including at the subsequent 1994 World Cup finals in the USA. Romania coasted through the early rounds and looked like being the only team that could challenge Brazil for the title. But they then succumbed to self-doubt and contrived to lose the quarter-final against a much less gifted Sweden. The reliably zany centre-forward, Florin Radicoiu, best explained the mindset that had brought about this failure by pronouncing that the Romanians: 'Were bound to lose because the Swedes have been eating bananas since they were three and we never had any'.

Bananas were a national obsession in Romania. They had just begun to appear on the nation's market stalls for the first time and shone like gold bars amongst the rotten apples and mouldy cabbages. The new wonder fruit was way out of the price range of most people. As a consequence, they took on a mythical status as a miraculous stimulant of health and wealth, not least for those selling them.

Radicoiu's outburst combined this folk wisdom with the severe inferiority complex that had taken root under Ceausescu's regime. While many people in the West believed the Cold War propaganda about hordes of fanatical, Stakhanovite supermen bursting through the Iron Curtain, most Romanians had witnessed the grinding reality of East European communism's failings every day of their lives. After decades of awful food, crumbling infrastructure and shoddy or non-existent goods, few regular people were under any illusion about the supposed superiority of the system they suffered under. Reliable information about the West was scarce but many people suspected that their counterparts there must be better off. Their suspicions about Westerners comparative lives of luxury were confirmed when the Berlin Wall fell. In Romania, this led to an assumption for years afterwards that everything Western was automatically superior to anything Romanian. For the national team at the 1994 World Cup, this belief also applied to Swedish footballers, despite the mountain of on-field evidence to the contrary.

At least Radicoiu never wanted for bananas again, as he subsequently secured a lucrative move to RCD Espanyol in Spain. At some point after his arrival in Barcelona, he apparently became convinced that there was a language requirement for obtaining Spanish citizenship that meant he must not get caught speaking any other language. This misconception led to the odd spectacle of him seemingly insisting on being interviewed on Romanian television in broken Spanish via an interpreter.

The opening up of moves to rich clubs in Western Europe was a personal boon for the players of Romania's best ever team. It did, though, kill any further chance of the team reaching the international heights. Some, such as the last of Europe's great liberos, Ghica Popescu, achieved professional success, captaining Barcelona, as well as prosperity. But most, like the electric striker, Ilie Dumitrescu, had their edge dulled by the unexpected avalanche of affluence and never fulfilled their potential.

Back at Ghencea in 1992, though, Dumitrescu was still the coming man. I discovered this at half-time in the Wales game when my attempts to get up in search of more delicious pickled veg were thwarted by an unprovoked pile-on by scruffy blokes with microphones. Engrossed in the game, I had not noticed that the injured Ilie was sitting in the seat behind me and I spent the next ten minutes being used as a step ladder by journalists scrambling up from the press box below to interview him during the break.

Fortunately, going home with boot prints up my VIP chest did nothing to tarnish the occasion. I was thoroughly hooked and made sure to rustle up a minibus trip from the Embassy for anything resembling a big game in future.

Our first such excursion was to a European Cup Winners' Cup tie between Steaua and the Danish club, Brondby.

Clearly we looked more Danish than Romanian, as we got the full minibus rocking experience on the way down Boulevard Ghencea. This unnerved some of my more delicate diplomatic colleagues. Even for me, a veteran follower of English football through the hooligan infested 'seventies and 'eighties, it was still a bit hair-raising.

Fortunately our local driver, Titi Niculescu, had the good sense to wind down the window, wave a Steaua scarf and shout: 'British! British Steaua fans!' to the throng out in the smoky gloom. This immediately alleviated the risk of seasickness, as the minibus was now becalmed and, after some polite requests for bananas, provoked a chant of, 'Souness, Souness!' from the crowd. Numerous cans of beer and handfuls of cigarettes were passed out of the windows, which secured us a place as guests of honour at the head of a cacophonous convoy for the rest of the way down the boulevard.

This experience was an indication of how the Romanian crowds' flair for intimidation was more knowing than fanatical.

It was all part of a ritual calculated to play on the opposition's trepidation at having stepped into the unknown. From the other side of the fence, once you were in the crowd, it was all friendly and conspiratorially silly.

I was regularly told with a grin to be quiet when a favourite trick was about to be perpetrated against a visiting substitute. The first instinct of most subs was that Ghencea was the sort of ground where one warmed up within a 20 centimetre radius of the covered dugout. Spotting this, the crowd on that side would go quiet and studiously ignore the sub. Slowly their dupe would become bolder and start extending his warm up exercises further down the touchline. Eventually he would reach the corner flag, far from the sanctuary of the bench. At this point the crowd would explode in derision and bombard their victim with fruit peel and cardboard sunflower seed holders as he launched into a hamstring busting sprint back to the dugout.

Much the same ritualistic approach was adopted to stadium security.

We discovered early on from bitter experience that the young, bedraggled conscript soldiers on duty had orders to prevent anyone from bringing bottles and cans of beer in through the turnstiles, or rusty gate as it actually was. But they clearly had no instructions to stop you standing ten metres away passing entire cases of ale over the perimeter fence to your mates who had already entered the ground and raised no objection to that at all. This came in handy because my friends and I soon discovered that Boddington's draught flow cans shared the social accelerant properties of bananas when making new Romanian friends. As foreigners with beer to share we stuck out in the Ghencea stands and were quickly welcomed as part of the scene.

Some notions become clichés because they happen to

be true and my experiences at Rapid and Steaua provided a memorable confirmation of sport's fabled ability to break down barriers between people.

Well, sport, bananas and free ale anyway.

9. Hello Dubai

THE down side of my posting in Bucharest was that it finished far too soon. Danny and my predecessors had been both surly and semi-competent. That was fortunate for us because it set the bar for looking good very low. It also disposed our senior colleagues to indulge our excesses because we were still helpful even when hungover, and they found it a relief to be around cheerful people who were obviously enjoying themselves. The snag was that my work performance led to me getting promoted after less than a year and a half. The Diplomatic Service structure operates on a system of grades, with each officer and job having a fixed ranking. Getting promoted from Diplomatic Service Grade 10 to DS9 meant that I had to move on from the Registry and away from Bucharest.

The reaction of my friends, colleagues and acquaintances when my second posting was announced was the mirror image of what it had been when I was posted to Romania. The consensus was that I had struck gold in landing Dubai – the best, most liberal place in the Gulf – I was told. I realised soon after I had actually got there that this was akin to describing someone as the world's tallest pygmy.

But at the time of my appointment, I could not find any logical grounds to disagree. Three years of sun, sand and luxury certainly sounded like hitting the jackpot.

Emotionally, though, the prospect of going to Dubai left me cold. I could not identify any concrete reasons for my trepidation and put it down to my disappointment at leaving Romania and, as I was to spend the next few years discovering, most of the reasons I acquired for loathing Dubai were based more on its atmosphere and my temperament than hard facts.

Dubai certainly looked nice on the glossy paper and brochures published by its tourism and investment authorities. The images of lots of shiny, happy people having fun in exotic places created an impression of some sort of desert Disneyland for grown-ups. In short, that was one of the main problems. Living the kind of life I was parachuted into there is akin to permanently living in a 5-star hotel. It's lovely for about two weeks but then the artifice becomes insidious and the shallowness starts to grate. After that you start to spot the rot beneath the surface.

But I should insert a caveat. I'd not strayed far enough from my roots to have completely lost perspective. In the end, living and working in the British Embassy in Dubai was well down the difficulty scale from crewing a North Sea fishing trawler. Even at its worst points, there was always the option of walking out of the front door and going to sit in the sun by the pristine swimming pool with a book, so it was not exactly unendurable. Then again, beliefs in fairness and dignity instilled from my background were part of what led me to dislike the place so much.

Dubai was little more than a fishing and pearl-diving village until around the late 1950s when the Emirates started capitalising on its oil resources. Indeed, the remnants of those earlier days near the mouth of the creek that bisects the city contain perhaps the only bits of authentic charm it has to offer. From the '60s onwards, and accelerating from the 1980s, a new city mostly consisting of fancy hotels and shopping centres was constructed. At first acquaintance, it was quite impressive to the urban-inclined like me, especially down by the creek where the gleaming glass facades reflected the sun and the waterfront. But it soon became apparent that there was not much behind them and one gleaming glass and marble lobby quickly began to seem much like another.

Aside from the architecture, the nature of the society impacted Dubai's absence of atmosphere and identity. Rapid development demanded the recruitment of masses of foreign workers at all levels. The demographic result was that the Emiratis became a small minority, about 12 per cent, of the population in their own country. One did meet them reasonably often, usually through work, and they were invariably pleasant and polite. But getting to know them better than that was difficult. Cultural traditions made contact with the female half of the population difficult in any case and the men were rarely inclined to move beyond professional acquaintance. The Emiratis were already family-orientated and had seemingly decided to focus inwardly in order to preserve their way of life. Given the peculiar nature of the society, I found that completely understandable. Unfortunately, the consequence was that a place where the local culture was hidden behind the high walls of the family villa lacked atmosphere in its public spaces.

They were mostly filled up by the rest of the population – the 88 per cent who were foreigners. Almost all of them had three-year employment and residence permits. They were issued completely at the behest of the employer and conveyed no independent rights of residence whatsoever. Of course, many people obtained permit renewals and stayed longer. But the fact that they could be revoked instantly on the whim of the employer created an insecure, transitory air that was an appropriate fit for a place that felt like a giant airport transit lounge.

Dubai proudly boasted that it was cosmopolitan, and it was in the narrow sense that its foreign residents came from many countries, particularly Asia, Europe and the Middle East. But they did not mix much and there was an ugly gradation of society into ranks based on ethnic and national origin. The Emiratis and other Gulf Arabs, were ranked above the incomers, to all intents and purposes beyond the law and any other social rules, particularly when it came to a dispute with a foreigner. Westerners came next and were generally all too willing to lord it over those deemed below them. They were joined at roughly the same level by a small number of other Middle Easterners who had lived in Dubai for a long-time as big business owners or, more accurately, minority shareholders in big companies, as all businesses in the Emirates, from multinationals to the corner shop, had to be 51 per cent owned by a local national. That was even if he played no greater role in its activities than signing his name on the trading licence and banking his percentage of the profits. There then followed a professional class of doctors - many Emiratis take their medical treatment outside the country, so doctors are not as valued as in most countries - engineers and middle managers from places like Egypt, Iraq and India.

Way down at the bottom of the pile was a mass of workers, often in construction, and domestic servants, usually from the Indian sub-continent and South-East Asia, who were treated appallingly. They were viewed, when they were considered at all, to be a completely expendable and inexhaustible resource. These workers were usually paid less than a thousand pounds a year, some of which would be siphoned off by the employment agent that brought them to Dubai. They were accommodated in either bare concrete or tented out-of-town camps in the baking desert with a handful of basic toilet and washing facilities shared between several hundred people. Even if they had had the means to do so, they were restricted from leaving their de facto detention camps and transported to and from work crammed into open-backed lorries that the Emiratis would not have allowed their camels in. In the case of the building workers, safety standards on the construction sites were rudimentary to non-existent. Deaths and injuries were common.

Such workers were all from very poor backgrounds. None of them expected to live in a posh beachside villa. They had come to graft hard and save money to build a better future for the families at home that they would not see from one year to the next. But given that Dubai was filthy rich and that the projects they were working on would make millions for the developers, there was absolutely no need for them to be treated so callously. Providing minimally decent safety and living standards would have made no discernible difference to the profit margins. Rather than hard-nosed economic calculation, the inherent disdain was the product of pure contempt on the part of people who considered themselves superior human beings.

The treatment of some domestic servants was even more sinister. Some were forced to work all hours, every day without a break and had their minimal wages withheld on the slightest pretext. As with the building workers, their passports would be kept by their employer to prevent them from escaping. And if you chose to dig deeper, it got even worse. The wives of two of my Indian colleagues were nurses at local hospitals. Once I got to know them better, they would nervously tell stories of housemaids who had suffered horrific sexual and other physical abuse at the hands of their Emirati employers. When these women were brought in, the nurses were instructed to patch them up sufficiently to be despatched back to Asia and sworn to secrecy by their managers on pain of their own jobs and continued residence in Dubai. There was never any question of any sanctions being taken against the employer, who remained free to recruit more maids to defile.

The majority of employers did not of course actively mistreat anyone. But almost all of us in the better off strata of Dubai society, and I include myself in this as the employer of a part-time cleaner, were happy to take unquestioning advantage of the availability of cheap, rights-free labour to make our already pampered lives that bit easier still. Most British expatriates found it easy to ignore the way these workers were treated and routinely referred to them in disparaging, racist terms. Others, who worked in more senior roles in the worst-offending industries, were more complicit in the abuses or at least managed to rationalise them as just being 'the way of the world' and beyond their control.

I found a lot not to like about Dubai but the British expat community saw off some stiff competition to become the biggest bane of my life there.

Perhaps I focused on them unfairly because, working in the Embassy, I came into contact with them much more than any other national group. There were, of course, some decent people amongst them who were there for career reasons and managed to enjoy the high material standard of living without being thrown off-kilter by the artificiality. But the place attracted more nasty pieces of work from Britain than anywhere else I have ever set foot in. Worse still, it had a knack for turning otherwise ordinary, decent people into shallow, arrogant idiots.

The head-inflating process often started with the ludicrous job titles people were given there. A white British plumber would, by virtue of his race and nationality, be put in charge of a team of twenty from the sub-continent, regardless of whether he had any management experience, or even superior plumbing skills. He would then be called something like Chief Executive Sanitary Engineer and addressed unfailingly as sir by his underlings. As part of his remuneration, he would be paid much more than he had ever earned elsewhere and be given a nice house and flash car. The house would come equipped with people from poorer countries to clean, fetch and carry, who also called them sir or madam. The opulence, excess and vanity simply increased in scale the further you looked up the employment chain.

Some particularly well-balanced people could cope with understanding the flummery for the nonsense it was and appreciated the material comforts. The majority, though, let it go completely to their heads and quickly slipped into an infuriating state of do-you-know-who-I-am arrogance. Rather than appreciating their new-found affluence and status, many people became tediously obsessed by it. It probably did not help that Dubai was almost maniacally dedicated to producing wealth or the illusion of it and had no political or cultural life alongside it. It did have some sport but most of this – golf, horse racing and powerboating was really just an extension of the need for greed and general ostentation.

In my more charitable moments, I fleetingly felt sorry for some of these expats, who had turned into people that even their families and old friends must have struggled to stomach. But this feeling usually dissipated at the first refrain of: 'Have you seen my huge new villa in Jumeirah' or, 'What is my Embassy doing for me?' The latter was frequently heard when expats came in for some routine reason and threw a hissy fit at having to speak to a, 'bloody Indian' on the reception counter. The fact that the Indian (some of whom were also British) had been performing the service they required fifty times a day for fifteen years did not seem to come into it. Nor did the notion, frequently muttered under my breath, that we might have been able to employ more staff from the UK if these ex-pats actually paid any of the rates that funded us, rather than living tax-free in Dubai.

As the Vice-Consul, constant contact with them was unavoidable. The difficulties of accessing the local culture and my limited imagination at the time meant that I also found it difficult to avoid their social scene.

I have often found, on overseas postings, that playing football was a good way to meet like-minded and interesting people of different nationalities. Up to a point, this worked in Dubai too. Through joining the well-established Creek FC, I met, for example, José, an amiably laid-back Spanish lad, a friendly Lebanese, Ragheb and a Palestinian called Khamis.

I first encountered Khamis, who played for another club, when I volunteered to drive him to hospital to get a nasty head wound, sustained in a game I was not playing in, stitched up. From his subsequent reaction, you would have thought that I had personally re-attached all four of his severed limbs. He was a fantastic bloke and for the next couple of years, I received endless hospitality from him, including a copious weekly delivery of the finest nuts and dried fruit from his food merchant brother. My only misgiving related to his German wife whose vociferous anti-Israeli opinions sometimes strayed beyond what was understandable for the spouse of a Palestinian refugee from

Gaza, and made her sound like a newsreel report from 1930's Berlin.

But, ultimately, interesting characters were a rarity because, in keeping with the informal segregation that characterised Dubai, Creek was a predominantly British club in a predominantly British league. It featured a few decent players and people such as the outstanding Chris Anderson, a man so grounded that he had turned down a professional contract with Sunderland to train as an accountant instead. But they were the exception. Ragheb's modest comprehension of English was exploited by his mostly repulsive British team-mates, who snidely corrupted his name to 'Rag Head'. These included the unpredictably violent Jimmy McLean, who was a sociopathic racist and misogynist. I could easily picture Jimmy back home as a sadistic knife-wielding sidekick of a drug baron. In Dubai, he was a mid-ranking executive for the Disney Corporation.

The club was also full of those who might have been regular people at home but whose heads had been inflated to beach ball proportions by life in Dubai.

The cock-of-the-walk at Creek FC was Dean Prince. It was easy to picture Dean as a cheerful London used-car salesman with the gift of the gab that he undoubtedly was at home. But in Dubai he was Vice-President of Automobile Merchandising Operations, with a worshipful sales team and it got to him. He was at a party at my house one night loudly comparing it unfavourably to his villa, while drinking my beer. Suddenly his quiet and unassuming wife collapsed unconscious behind him, crashing her head sickeningly against the floor tiles. She had been discreetly knocking back industrial quantities of gin all night. She was a not uncommon example of a capable, independent woman with a close circle of family and friends being brought to the Gulf as a trailing spouse and ending up self-medicating through the shallow existence of tedious coffee-morning conversations in the gilded cage.

I sympathised totally with Mrs Prince's apparent need for an anaesthetic against the awfulness of Dubai. While I never quite matched the commitment of Nicolas Cage in *Leaving Las Vegas* by pledging to drink myself to death in a similarly nauseating, neon-lit, plastic hellhole, the outcome of my approach to life there could have been much the same.

I had been 'blessed' with a large capacity for alcohol from an early stage. Even by the sky-high standards of Hull, I was a pioneer of binge-drinking long before it became fashionable. This practice continued in London and Bucharest. The difficulty I faced now was that my motivation for it had, unthinkingly, switched from pleasure to escapism. My lack of an off-switch combined with a dearth of people in Dubai that I enjoyed talking to accelerated my imbibing pace from already brisk to warp speed. At this point, having hollow legs and endless stamina to keep pouring it in ceased to work in my favour.

During my first year in Dubai, the merging of Thursday and Friday nights, the local weekend, into one drunken haze followed by memory loss became commonplace, although some of the gaps would occasionally be filled in with a mixture of horror and admiration by my acquaintances the next time I saw them. Sometimes complete strangers would approach me with tales of evenings spent in their company, of which I had no recollection.

For all of my adventures in extreme inebriation, I can at least say that I was rarely given to putting others in danger by drink-driving, which was an epidemic amongst some of my diplomatic colleagues. There was one occasion in the Emirates when I appalled myself by failing to meet even this standard of basic social responsibility, involving a short spell of terror when I woke up late in the morning stinking of chlorine and covered in sand. All I could remember was being at a football tournament on a packed sand-pitch in the nearby Emirate of Sharjah the previous day. My team had successfully got knocked out in the first round, freeing us up for a full day of boozing in the sun. The next piece of the jigsaw seemingly fell into place when I sniffed the chlorine, spotted my car keys on the floor and recalled that my allocated parking space back in Dubai was separated from the compound's swimming pool by only a couple of yards of patio and a flimsy hedge. Clearly I must have driven home and parked the Saab in the shallow end.

I was already mentally packing my bags and contemplating an afternoon flight home in disgrace when a colleague let herself in through the unlocked door of my house next to the Embassy to find out why I had not turned up for work. She was prevailed upon to go across the compound to confirm the damage. Mercifully, she reported back that whilst my car was parked at an odd angle with the windows open and sand clogging the wheel arches, there was no sign of it having taken a dip. A few discreet phone calls then established that my last act in Sharjah had been to fall into the football club's swimming pool on my way back from the bar, before disappearing into the night. I had then presumably somehow driven back down the motorway to Dubai via an off road detour into the desert by the side of the road.

Apart from inbuilt stupidity, an element of shyness and not having the wit at that age to do something else with my evenings, the drinking issues I developed in Dubai were enhanced by an unconscious desire to escape the stifling, money-driven conformity of ex-pat life and the tediously fake environment.

Ironically, the pubs where I spent much of my time trying to make my escape epitomised this falseness. They were all mock-ups of the kind of establishments the developers imagined you would find in places that actually had real pubs and bars, mostly in Britain, Ireland and, for some odd reason, Texas. Due to the licensing restrictions they all had to be located within hotel premises and only serve non-Muslim foreigners. No freestanding establishments were allowed to serve alcohol.

The only pushing of this boundary came in the case of the couple of large nightclubs, which were located in places with a token handful of unoccupied rooms and a hotel bar that resembled a super-sized Stringfellow's. The most popular of these establishments was The Highland Lodge, which could have more accurately been described as a cowshed. It was ex-pat hell but, nonetheless, I diligently went there most weekends during my first year, desperately trying to find something to like about Dubai and its denizens, whilst simultaneously nurturing my excess.

The news bulletins of the time were dominated by reports of Serbian rampages through the former Yugoslavia. But to a large extent, I was saved by the Serbs. Somehow, late one evening in the other main nightclub, The Cyclone, I slurred comprehensibly enough to get the phone number of Lilja Vrbancic, an attractive Serbian textile designer who became my long-term girlfriend and whose eye I had apparently caught when issuing her a visa a few weeks earlier. Or more accurately ear – she was inordinately impressed by my ability to pronounce her vowel starved surname correctly in a strangely appealing Hull accent.

Lilja was one of a small community of engagingly bohemian Yugoslavs who had fled from the war in their homeland caused by nationalists with whom they had no affinity. Unlike most of my compatriots in Dubai, they were open-minded and stimulating people to be around, with a wide range of professional, cultural and political interests. Even in their company, Lilja stood out as a livewire. Her liberal European attitudes, which included sharing a flat with her ex-husband, Dusan, who somehow always felt comfortable for her boyfriend to visit, were a refreshing contrast to the overt primness that abounded. Although she was no model of wholesome clean living herself, Lilja, to my eternal gratitude, provided distraction enough to divert me from total booze-fuelled self-destruction.

I did come close. Dusan once described me as: 'The drunkest man in the world'. For someone who had never been top of the class in anything, this felt like quite a compliment, particularly because he had not exactly led a sheltered existence and knew what he was talking about. Unusually amongst the Yugoslavs, his exile in Dubai had not been prompted by the war. Instead, he had found it prudent to put some distance between him and an organised crime boss from whom he had borrowed money to open a nightclub in Belgrade, which had produced more fun than profits.

Apart from Lilja, Dubai had a few redeeming chinks of light - singing along to Country Road with the Manila Cowboys house band in the Filipino bar notwithstanding - that kept enough of my spirits alive to scrape through my time there. On the social scene, months of careful research and pestering taxi-drivers paid off when I finally managed to locate some enjoyable venues away from the European mainstream. One scruffy, low budget hotel had the tiny, sweaty African Club hidden away in its basement. It was absolutely brilliant, with an exuberant Zimbabwean band and a diverse range of lively punters. The crowd was enlivened further every few weeks by a huge and extravagantly gay US naval officer enjoying a boisterous evening out while his ship was in port. I got to know him well during a series of uproarious nights that resembled being on the road with the Village People.

The African Club did have a couple of hazards. The first was the location of the gents' toilets right next to the dance floor. Every time the door opened, the bright lights within gave anyone interested a clear view of the goods on offer. As soon as you walked out, you would be greeted with either thumbs-up or humiliating wiggling little fingers. A thumbs-up was more gratifying but made getting a drink treacherous because it encouraged the ladies of the night who congregated around the bar to indulge in their idiosyncratic, below the belt handshake greeting.

Another great place was found behind a similarly scruffy hotel in Deira on the opposite side of town. This one actually had a small sign with a direction arrow above the street outside saying Garage, which must have caused passing motorists untold confusion. The interior was inspired by the set of the classic 1970s TV series *Taxi*, with New York yellow cabs turned into convertibles with tables in the middle and the DJ in the Danny DeVito booth. It was particularly popular with South East Asians and played a lot of disco-ed up Elvis tracks that they loved. It was also distinguished by its smattering of gay Emiratis wearing their traditional immaculate white dishdasha robes with neatly trimmed beards, full make-up and bright red fingernails. They provided an eye-opening alternative image of the superficially straight-laced society from which they came.

Dubai did, at least, offer plenty of opportunities to get out of the place, with its numerous direct flights to a wide range of locations. The trouble I had in taking advantage was that it was difficult for me to be off work because I was the Embassy's only Visa Officer and the Visa Section had to close when I was not there. Consequently, all of my holidays came in a single four week chunk when a temporary replacement was sent out. By the time my annual break came around I was usually desperate to get as far away from the Emirates as possible and ended up seeing embarrassingly little of the wider region during my three years there. There were places in the Persian Gulf that could easily be reached for a weekend. But, as we were not allowed to go to or via Iran, this basically left a bunch of similar destinations. Occasionally, I liked going down the motorway to Abu Dhabi - being in Dubai never felt better than when you had just returned from a day in even more miserable, uptight location.

The other option for a few hours solace was to drive up to the more obscure Northern Emirates. Tiny Umm-al-Qawain was mildly interesting in that it had apparently slept through the last two centuries. If you squinted a bit against the bright sun shining on the white dusty sand, you could imagine that you were in an Arab version of *A Fistful of Dollars*. Umm-al-Qawain was like a ghost town, with ancient wooden doors creaking on their hinges and banging into their frames while tumbleweed blew down the sandy streets.

I did experience my own high noon just up the coast in Ras Al-Khaimah. For want of something better to do, a colleague, Martin Robinson, and I decided to drive up there on a whim one weekend morning. We didn't find anything of interest in the town because most of it was closed. We got in the car to head back and a few miles out we spotted a kerfuffle going on a short distance from the main road in the scrubland near some rocky hills. There were dozens of four wheel drives, some big tents, people milling about and a general hubbub drifting through the air. After a day distinctly lacking in thrills, we were overcome with excitement at having apparently stumbled on the drama of a car boot sale, or even a camel auction, and decided to pull off to take a look.

As we drove up to the gathering, it seemed we had made a bad decision. We were rapidly surrounded by a large group of fearsome looking men in traditional dress, chanting vociferously and firing rifles into the air. At a time when several Western hostages were being held in the Middle East, our immediate sense of unease was understandable. Retreat was cut off and the leader of the group motioned us to get out of the car with the barrel of his gun. We were then marched at the head of the posse into the central marquee, realising with horror that neither of us had told anyone back in Dubai where we were going.

The mood changed when were greeted effusively by everyone in it, including our erstwhile captors. What we had stumbled upon was a traditional men-only wedding party – the Emirati equivalent of a stag night. The unannounced arrival of strangers was considered to be the ultimate good luck sign for the groom. Consequently, the welcoming committee had opted for ruthlessness when they saw our nervous faces and abortive attempts to engage reverse gear. They then spent the rest of the day demonstrating that they were in fact hospitality terrorists. We were force-fed all manner of delicious food, including freshly, and loudly, slaughtered meat grilled on an open fire, until way beyond the point where making a run for it had become a physical impossibility.

The scent of danger never disappeared entirely because, as the guests of honour, we were seated opposite the toothless, doddery and voluble family patriarch. He had the alarming habit of cleaning his shotgun every five minutes with his shaky hands and waving it vigorously in our direction whenever he was making a point. When we were finally permitted to leave, long after nightfall and accompanied by another cacophony of firing into the air, we had enjoyed the rare opportunity to witness these apparently aloof and austere people banging drums, dancing, laughing and generally having a whale of a time.

10. Peacocks and Prisoners

IN between the nightlife, there was still work to be done. The most instantly appealing aspect of my new job as Vice-Consul was the living arrangements. The house with which I was provided was located on the verdant, Creek-side Embassy compound, a few steps from the pool and tennis court. Perhaps its only downside was its peacock population. Their beauty was tarnished by their ungodly squawking and habit of wandering into my living room to crap on the carpet whenever the patio door was open.

I eventually found a cure for the invasions. One weekend day I put some eggs on to boil for lunch and promptly forgot about them, heading off for a leisurely trip to the supermarket to pick up some shopping before my parents arrived from the UK later that evening on a visit. Unthinkingly, I stopped for a bite to eat and then decided to run another couple of errands too. By the time I got home several hours later, the house was filled with smoke and I rapidly remembered why. I ran into the kitchen, extracted the smoking remnants of the pan and rushed outside with it, putting it down in a panic on the plastic patio table to cool off. The pan melted into the table but the upside was that the smell of burning plastic and sulphur lingered in my house for the next six months, totally putting off the peacocks - and any other house guests it must be said - from entering.

My house was not only attractively located, it was in a converted wing of the Embassy building, with my bedroom and office sharing an adjoining wall. Memories of London commuting were still fresh in my mind when I arrived in Dubai and the elimination of the journey to work seemed like a promising sign. I was quickly disabused of this when I discovered that the potential for lying-in was negated by the Embassy start time of seven thirty in the morning.

Fortunately, that problem was also easy to solve. Most mornings I would get up minutes before the start time, dress quickly and go into the Embassy via the main entrance at the far end of the building from my front door. Then, having paused ostentatiously to say good morning and advertise my punctuality to the strict Deputy Head of Mission, Jim Finlay, I would continue down the corridor to my office, climb on to the air conditioning unit and jump out of the window into my back garden. This strategy enabled me to go home for a shower and breakfast before slipping back in through the fire exit at eight to greet my first customers of the day.

My main role in Dubai was to make decisions on an annual, average 15,000 visa applications from foreign nationals wishing to travel to the UK. Visa Sections are generally perceived as being the least glamorous departments of our diplomatic missions overseas but often have a high public profile. The citizens of over one hundred countries do not have luxury of travelling to the UK at will. They must first obtain a visa from a British Embassy permitting them to enter whether to visit, study or live there long-term.

The requirement to obtain a visa is a sensitive subject because it is a restraint on freedom and can easily be perceived as imputing a lesser status to people of some nationalities. In practical terms, applying for a visa is also expensive, time consuming and a potentially frustrating bureaucratic exercise.

Consequently, the courtesy and efficiency with which applications are processed has a far greater impact on the image of the UK in most countries than high-level political negotiations or any of the other more exalted activities in which an Embassy is involved. A breakdown in the visa processing system can be front page news in some countries. And the risk of system failure is high.

It is a struggle to resource our Visa Sections adequately in a globalised world where the number of international travellers increases every year. This places considerable strain on the Visa Officers, who deal with hundreds of applicants every day, a minority of whom may be aggressive or dishonest. The pressure of the workload, coupled with the borderline hysteria about preventing illegal immigration that currently prevails in Britain, can cause them to develop an unbalanced approach. It is, of course, important to prevent bogus applicants from travelling to the UK. But seeing grounds for suspicion in almost every one causes the whole system to slow down. This leads to visas not being issued in time for honest travellers to make their flights or business appointments and creates an impression of the UK that does not welcome money-spending tourists or international business.

In fact, very few of our Visa Sections overseas refuse more than ten per cent of the visa applications they receive. The first priority for the Visa Officer, then, is to separate the vast majority of genuine applicants from the small number of risky ones and issue their visas quickly because our economy depends on foreign trade and tourism. Despite its importance, senior Embassy staff are seldom keen to get involved in the messy slog of visa work, which involves making numerous difficult and personally sensitive decisions every day. High-flyers are also put off by the production line aspect of the repetitive work. Applicants are processed along a sequence of counters, where their paperwork is checked for the necessary supporting documents, payment processed and then their request finally judged, with the pursuant being interviewed, if necessary, before obtaining their objective or finding a refusal stamp inserted in their passport.

I was fortunate that my turn at visa work came in Dubai. Apart from during the two months of the summer rush, when applications spiked as people sought to escape the stifling heat and humidity of the Emirates, the workload there was more varied. Every day brought a multi-coloured pile of passports from the wide range of visa-requiring nationals with their diverse backgrounds, circumstances and reasons for travel.

Rather than the applicants, my biggest initial challenge was managing a team that expanded up to seventeen staff during the hectic summer months. I had no previous experience and quickly had to work out how to handle an eclectic group of colleagues which included the tough Deputy Head of Mission's wife and a kaleidoscope of nationalities, religious and cultural backgrounds. Almost inevitably, some of them were prone to petty squabbles and constantly vying to convince the new, young boss to take their side. Dropping me into this intensive situation was typical of the Foreign Office's enduring and often surprisingly effective 'gentleman amateur' approach to staff deployment, which relied a lot on figuring it out on the job.

I was sent on a short management training course, based off-site at a hotel in wintry Bournemouth, before deployment. It is probably more of a reflection on me than them that the only thing I remember is spending one evening living it up on complementary drinks in the VIP section of a local nightclub, having persuaded the management that a regal looking female colleague was the Princess of Luxembourg and the rest of us were her Foreign Office minders. I think we made the society pages of the local paper but fortunately the FCO Security Department must have missed the *Bournemouth Echo* that week.

Something more productive must have seeped in, though, and between the training and making it up as I went along, I managed to knit together a broadly cohesive team. I realised quickly that expecting total peace and harmony was unrealistic. Instead, allowing each of them to let off steam once in a while in my office was a good way of averting unseemly arguments featuring all manner of regional, religious and cultural slurs, from breaking out in the public areas of the Section.

I am sure the Embassy hierarchy must have had misgivings about London's decision to replace their two experienced visa officers with one newly promoted 22-year-old. But in fact the cautious approach of at least one of my predecessors made it easy for me to institute some rapid changes that reduced the processing time for routine visas from three days to one. My Head of Post, like most Ambassadors, was at his happiest with us when he was not receiving any complaints demanding his involvement and he received positive comments from the British and Emirati business community about the improvements. These were a welcome bonus and made me appear to be some sort of whiz kid. Not for the first time, I had discovered that the best jobs to get were ones that offered easy scope for looking good by comparison with ones predecessors.

Streamlining the processing of the straightforward visa applications opened up more time for dealing with the less simple cases. The key to handling the difficult ones was acquiring a good knowledge of the place, its inhabitants and their circumstances. It enabled you to make an informed judgement on whether people were likely to return and if their declared reason for travel was logical.

Sometimes, though, these familiar indicators went out of the window and some flexibility was required. For example, we regularly received applications to travel for fertility treatment at private clinics from Iranians who were not resident in Dubai and had travelled across the Gulf to apply with us because the British Embassy in Tehran only operated a restricted visa service. Most of these were not well-off and had never left home before. My sketchy knowledge about life in Iran and the near impossibility of obtaining reliable supporting documents about employment, family and financial circumstances made it difficult at first to make an informed judgement. In time, though, I was able to develop a feel for such requests and ended up issuing visas to almost all of them. It quickly became apparent that infertility was not a story that was often used by Iranians seeking to cheat the immigration system. In these specific circumstances, a culture which prized having children more than most meant that those proposing to spend every penny they had, on travelling to a place about which they knew nothing, were usually entirely genuine in their intentions.

Some other medical applications were less sensitive. One young, heavy-accented Indian woman came in every day for a week insisting that she needed to go to the UK for emergency medical treatment for a mysterious, life-threatening condition she called 'Ibilis' that could not be treated in Dubai. She matched all of the usual grounds for suspicion, which were only heightened by her demeanour and garbled story. On each occasion she was sympathetically informed that, in order to obtain a visa, she needed to bring a referral from her doctor, an appointment letter from a UK hospital outlining the treatment plan, cost and nature of her medical condition and some evidence that she could pay the doctor's bill. Eventually, at about the fifth attempt, she came in triumphantly brandishing a crumpled NHS information leaflet about 'IBS – Irritable Bowel Syndrome' instead. That solved the mystery surrounding her ailment but, sadly, still fell someway short of providing the supporting evidence required to issue her with a visa under the Immigration Rules.

The other awkward, although frequent, applications were for permanent settlement in the UK as a wife or husband of a British citizen. The Visa Officer had to assess whether such marriages were genuine or being entered into simply to facilitate immigration. At one end of the scale, there were couples who had clearly been living their married life together overseas for several years. They simply needed to demonstrate that they had adequate means of supporting themselves in Britain without recourse to public funds.

The more complicated ones involved arranged marriages originating from the Indian sub-continent. Often, the couple had not met more than once and had yet to build up a substantive relationship. The actual immigration applicant was frequently from a poor background, usually in the same region from which the previous generations had emigrated legally decades earlier. Such circumstances made it difficult in the extreme to establish whether the applicant satisfied the 'primary purpose' rule that was in force at the time, which decreed that the request should be refused if the main motivation for the marriage was economic advancement. In practice, this vague principle was almost impossible to interpret fairly, irrespective of geography, religion or lifestyle.

We also frequently had to deal with marriage visa applications from Filipina or Thai women in low-paid, usually domestic staff, occupations. They demanded careful judgement, the unenviable financial, living and employment circumstances of these women meant that they could hardly have been blamed if they had entered into a sham marriage purely for economic advancement and as a means to gain entry to the UK. Sometimes their proposed husbands were men who had limited marriage prospects and, to make the decision more complicated, some of these couples had only met a few times, having been put in touch via a marriage agency or a mutual friend.

Once any concerns about the British sponsor's ability to support his prospective spouse without recourse to social security payments had been allayed, the next task was to somehow uncover whether the relationship was genuine. Often the only way to do that was to ask for phone bill records and written correspondence between the applicants. I always found asking to read the private letters of a respectable woman perhaps ten years my senior deeply uncomfortable and prurient. I would be a liar, though, if I did not admit that it could sometimes be amusing.

Most applicants sensibly found a way to edit the letters they chose to present and withhold those with the most intimate content – as we always made clear, the purpose of the request was to establish that there was a genuine relationship with regular communication, not pry into the most personal details of it. But one plump, middle-aged, rather conservative looking Filipina lady responded by presenting an impressive pile of correspondence with her fiancé that readers of *Fifty Shades of Grey* would have found overly erotic. The most recent missive from her prospective husband expressed his hope that she would receive her visa in time to join him at home for Christmas because he had purchased a skimpy Father Christmas suit for her. He went on to detail the fun that would ensue in front of the roaring fireplace when she came down the chimney wearing it. I did not have the heart to puncture the fantasy by explaining to the lady smiling sweetly in front of me that this scenario was going to be difficult to create in the static caravan he lived in in Llandudno. Nor did I have the heart to prolong the risk of either of them spontaneously combusting and issued the visa on the spot.

Perhaps the most disturbing visa case I was involved in there was that of a major Indian organised crime boss. He was one of a group of notorious individuals who had based themselves in Dubai because of the absence of an extradition treaty with India and the ample opportunities to launder their ill-gotten gains by purchasing hotels, nightclubs and other property in the no-questions-asked environment of the Emirates. Apart from being one of the world's biggest heroin traders, he was implicated in the carrying out of the 1993 Bombay bombings that killed over 250 people. He was taking a risk in attempting to travel to the UK because it raised the possibility of an extradition warrant being served on him while there.

I was tasked with using the guise of a routine visa interview to extract as much information as possible from the gangster about his finances and visit plans. In the meantime, his wife and children had already travelled to the UK on the visas we had issued them. The problem was that the Emirati authorities, seeing a chance to rid themselves of a problem, were refusing to renew the Dubai residence visas the family needed to return to the UAE. This left me in the bizarre position of sitting alone on several occasions in a small interview room with this terrifying individual, while he bawled his eyes out about being separated from his family and I feigned ignorance about the true reasons why I could not issue a visa to an ostensibly wealthy businessman. With hindsight, it might have been wise for me to have spent less time during this period in the nightclub he owned but, being young and daft, it never occurred to me.

Once I got over the natural inclination of extreme irritation from being lied to, I found it difficult to summon up any real dislike for applicants who tried to pull the wool over my eyes about their true intentions in applying for a visa. Most of them had been born into much more difficult circumstances, with many fewer opportunities, than I had. In all honesty, if the only chance to secure a better life for me and my family necessitated telling a few fibs to a faceless bureaucrat in an Embassy, then I might well have done it too. The job gave me a greater insight and understanding into humanity.

Indeed, I often wonder whether trying to uphold a total blockade against people who are frequently hard-working and resourceful is really the most sensible policy for Britain. There is much to commend the phrase uttered, in a rare fit of wisdom, by George W. Bush about illegal Mexican immigrants to the USA: 'Hell, if they'll walk across Big Bend (a notoriously dangerous border region) to get here, we want 'em'.

There were other aspects to my Vice-Consul job in Dubai beyond the workaday grind of processing thousands of visa applications. About once every three weeks I would be called by the Immigration & Customs Office at the airport to investigate a suspected case of passport fraud. We had trained the Emirati officers and check-in staff there to detect forged UK passports and they became pretty adept at spotting them.

The most common attempt involved inserting the bogus traveller's photograph into a passport stolen or bought from a genuine British citizen. Some of these attempts at substitution were easy to spot because getting the photo under the laminate and recreating the embossed symbols over the top of it was a tricky task. Others were a work of art and difficult to detect even with the specialised toolkit with which we were issued for the purpose. I often marvelled at the ingenuity that had gone into this nefarious task but the forged holder was usually picked up because the fraudster from whom he had bought his passport had devoted considerable attention to making the document look genuine but failed to equip his customer with a back story that would enable him to pass himself off as the real McCoy.

The fake passport holders I came across were almost all from only two countries, Bangladesh and Nigeria. Their typical responses to being caught could hardly have been more different. The Bangladeshis were invariably timid, slight young men being sent by their families to Britain to seek work in the restaurant trade. By the time I got to the airport, they were usually demoralised and terrified at having been detained and ready to go back to the home they had just left for the first time. It was impossible not to feel sorry for them. A desultory burst of the good cop/bad cop routine I had established with the Emirati officers, who did a convincing line in menacing, was usually enough to persuade the miscreant to tell all about how and why he had obtained the passport. All that was required was the promise of an early flight back to Bangladesh and not having to spend any more time alone with the large, moustachioed men in green uniforms.

The Nigerians were a different matter entirely. They usually had a story to tell, albeit a ludicrous one, and a determination to stick to it until the bitter end. One young woman began by berating me aggressively about the lack of assistance she was receiving from, 'my Embassy'. The problem was that she was clearly at least twenty years younger than the real owner of the passport and insisted that her supposed place of birth, Poole, or Poo-lay as she pronounced it, was in North London. She was eventually escorted onto a flight back to Lagos, minus the forged passport, still shouting indignantly that she was, 'a Christian lady' who would be writing to the BBC and the Queen about her unjust treatment. On another occasion, a Nigerian man put up a similarly spirited defence of his preposterous story for about an hour of fruitless questioning before startling us by declaring emphatically that: 'I think you have proved that I am a liar. Please may I go home to Nigeria?'

People skills were at a premium in the non-visa part of my job too. Along with two of my colleagues, I provided consular assistance to British citizens. My main task was to make welfare visits to Brits in prison in Dubai and the Northern Emirates. Contrary to the hopes and expectations of some, Consuls do not have the power to intervene in the legal process and engineer freedom. Our role was to do what we could to ensure that they were receiving humane treatment, as well as access to a lawyer, medicines, post and parcels from home and so on.

This role brought me into contact with some distressing cases. Our restricted to welfare remit meant that there was no real value in making judgements about the prisoner's guilt or innocence but on some occasions it was impossible not to take a view and led to us pushing the scope of our role to the limit. One of my long-term cases was a lad in his late teens whose parents were living in the Emirates. He had accepted a lift home from a nightclub one evening from some other young people he had just met. The car had been stopped by the police and a small, quantity of cocaine was found in one of the rear seat pockets. Even the court judgement accepted that there was no proof that the drugs belonged to the young Brit in question. Indeed, the driver of the car, a Latin American who obtained bail in murky circumstances and skipped the country, later admitted that they belonged to him. But the ludicrously draconian anti-narcotics laws in the Emirates meant that the young man was still sentenced to three years imprisonment just for being in the car when the drugs were found.

The detainee had even worse luck in that he was holed up in an atrocious old jail in Sharjah, rather than the more modern facility in Dubai. The prison was filthy, overcrowded and lacked the most basic amenities. Every time I visited him, his health seemed to have deteriorated alarmingly. His skin became disturbingly pale from not being permitted to go outside for weeks on end, despite the promises we elicited to the contrary from the prison governor. He was prisoner-of-war camp thin from the lousy food and constant stomach bugs. On each occasion, it seemed that he had acquired a new, septic and barely treated wound from some mishap or another. We discretely encouraged an excellent Lebanese lawyer who was well-known to the Embassy to take on the case on a pro-bono basis. By leaning on most of his extensive network of contacts, he eventually managed to get it reviewed and the poor kid released after eighteen months of his sentence.

Even where there was little doubt about the guilt of the prisoner, the circumstances could be deeply sad. There was one young woman who was serving a thirty year sentence in Dubai for heroin smuggling. She was hopelessly naïve and may have had learning difficulties. She'd grown up in the West Country with a single-parent mother who had plenty of problems of her own and little time for her daughter. Aged seventeen, she had met an older man who had wined and dined her before taking her on the trip of a lifetime to various destinations in South East Asia. He eventually gave her a bag to carry for him from Thailand via Dubai to Amsterdam, where she was meant to hand it over to his friend there.

The bag, of course, contained several kilos of heroin and she was arrested in transit. Our Embassy Drugs Liaison Officer, who worked on anti-narcotics operations with the Emirati authorities, was convinced that she had been set up as a decoy designed to distract the Customs' attention from another, more subtle smuggling operation. The scruffy and unworldly young woman had been sent in business class with no luggage apart from the offending bag and was a tailor-made candidate to be searched. None of this cut any ice with the Emirati authorities and she was destined to spend the bulk of her adult life in Dubai Womens' Prison without parole.

Fortunately, consular work was not all about misery. Local law in Dubai permitted polygamy which meant that marriages conducted there were not valid under UK law. Consequently, we had the unusual responsibility of conducting authorised wedding ceremonies in the Embassy. It was an oddly nerve-wracking experience, with the difficulty enhanced the first time I performed one because the bride was a stunning professional model in a very low-cut dress. Focusing on the script demanded an almighty feat of concentration as the beads of sweat glistened on her cleavage in the sweltering July heat.

Despite the offbeat nightclubs, near-death experiences, armed kidnapping, fraud, erotica, prisons, weddings, international terrorism and organised crime, Dubai was dull and did nothing for me. I could not wait to move on.

11. Uzbekis Where?

THE postings system of the increasingly people-friendly Foreign Office had changed by the time I was preparing to leave Dubai. Rather than the old league-ladders lottery, we were now given a full list of all of the jobs coming up and required to apply for six of them in preference order. Our bids were then assessed against those of our colleagues by a selection board made up of staff from around the Foreign Office. One of the main aims of the new system was to produce greater fairness by diminishing the power of Personnel Operations Department. They, though, were still able to steer the process because their role was to supply the board with information about each applicant and recommendations about where to post them.

My schedule contained some attractive potential ports of call such as Paris and Brasilia, which, of course, I put straight at the top of my wish list. It also included some intriguing oddities that I had to consider because the new system stipulated that we had to include at least two destinations that were categorised as difficult. For someone who had immensely enjoyed the posting everyone said I would detest and, assuming that anywhere would be better than where I now was, the choice was hardly off-putting. And the thought of obscure and exotic sounding places was what had attracted me to the Foreign Office in the first place.

In the end, I plumped for Minsk in Belarus and Tashkent in Uzbekistan as my lesser selections. I reasoned that I had liked Eastern Europe the last time around, so I might as well go the whole hog and try the former Soviet Union. Minsk and Tashkent also involved six months pre-posting Russian language training, which I fancied tackling because it seemed ridiculous to still be virtually monolingual after eight years in the Foreign Office.

Language training would also rectify a long-standing career handicap. On my first bewildering day in the Service, I had been asked to take, without any preparation or warning, a language aptitude test. Unbeknown to me, it was standard practice to spring it on new arrivals. The language used for the test, I discovered later, was Kurdish, which is one of the world's most difficult tongues. But I had been more confused by the unfamiliar audio equipment and absence of any prior instruction about what we were supposed to be doing. It passed in a blur and I bore a lingering grudge about the language aptitude assessment on my Personnel file indicating that I, 'might manage basic English after much careful instruction'.

Such a low rating hindered my chances of getting many of the jobs I desired because they often had a language learning requirement. My calculation was that the best way to destroy this damaging assessment was to seize the opportunity to learn a difficult language. Apart from that, getting paid to study one full-time for six months sounded like a good deal and the prospect of being able to speak Russian was way too cool to miss for a kid brought up during the Cold War.

My new Personnel Officer, Helen Morris, was also a personal friend. When she received my bidding form, she called me with barely disguised horror in her voice. Apparently Eastern Europe had not got any more popular over the years I had been away. 'Paul, I see you have got Tashkent on your list,' she said. 'I know you have to put some difficult posts on there but do you want me to cross that one out for you? Do you know that if you leave it in, you will get it?' Clearly it was great to get some more candid advice from Personnel than I had had earlier in my career. But, based on my experience so far, I realised that, yes, the job in the place that no-one else wanted was exactly what I would like to get next.

And so it came to pass. My first experience of the new selection board system was like getting one of those Christmas presents that you have already tried on for size and been told you are getting in mid-November. All I had to do then was find out where the hell Tashkent was exactly.

It would be an understatement to say that information about Uzbekistan was scarce. The handful of bookshops in Dubai were no use whatsoever. Even once I had returned to London to start my language training, the usually reliable treasure troves that were the Foreign Office library and the capital's travel bookshops had little on Central Asia beyond the odd ancient account of 'The Great Game', the 19th Century struggle for influence over the region that took place between Britain and Tsarist Russia. These tales of previous British envoys being imprisoned for years in bug-filled pits in Bukhara were all very interesting in an old-fashioned ripping yarns sort of way. But I wanted to learn more about what had gone on more recently.

I did manage to locate the country on the map. Although the Uzbeks, or at least their leaders, tend to see it as the centre of the universe, it is, as far as most people are concerned, pretty remote, effectively behind China, above Afghanistan and below the empty middle bit of Russia. But, given the vast distances involved, it is even further from the beaten track than that rough description makes it sound.

One of the few facts I unearthed is that it is the world's only double-landlocked country, meaning that it is totally surrounded by other landlocked countries, which is one to keep in mind for quiz night. On the map, I saw that Uzbekistan was shaped a bit like Italy, only with the boot rocking back on the heel, pointing the other way and kicking Kyrgyzstan up the arse. As I discovered later, this was politically as well as geographically accurate.

Nothing much of global significance had happened there since the Russian Empire took full control of the various Central Asian Khanates that covered the territory of present day Uzbekistan in the late-1800s. They were incorporated fairly seamlessly into the new Soviet Union after the 1917 revolution despite some resistance from local Basmachi guerrillas. A single Uzbek entity was carved out for the first time in 1924 and became one of the constituent republics of the Soviet Union. As with all of the others, the Uzbek Soviet Socialist Republic (SSR) suffered greatly during Stalin's purges and forced collectivisation of agriculture in the 1930s. It recast the Uzbek Republic as little more than a vast producer of cotton for the USSR, with terrible long-term environmental consequences. From then onwards, the place settled down to being one of the more obscure and docile of the Soviet Union's constituent parts.

Perhaps the Uzbek Republic's only glimpse above the parapet during the last six decades of the Soviet Union's existence was the Rashidov scandal in the 1980s. This case, with hindsight, offered perhaps the clearest indication of the rot in the USSR that would lead to its demise just a few years later.

Sharaf Rashidov was the local Communist Party boss and ran the place like a feudal lord. In 1984, it was revealed that he had been perpetrating a huge cotton harvest swindle. The production figures declared to the authorities running the Soviet Union's centrally planned economy in Moscow, on which transfers of central funds to the republics were based, had been massively falsified for years. Vast swathes of cotton fields had in fact been left empty and a sizeable percentage of the cotton that was actually produced was sold on the black market instead. Various senior Soviet officials who had been paid millions to protect Rashidov, including President Brezhnev's son-in-law, Yury Churbanov, were convicted of corruption and given long prison sentences. The managers of some state owned cotton enterprises were found to have been running them like the Khans and Emirs of old, operating virtual slave plantations with numerous concubines, private armies and torture chambers in the basement.

Rashidov was never prosecuted because it would have been too embarrassing for the Soviet leadership, even during Gorbachev's era of Glasnost. But he was eventually replaced by one of his loyal deputies, Islam Karimov. Karimov proved to be a chip off the old Rashidov block. As the Soviet Union sank in 1991, he attempted to cling on to the wreckage for as long as possible and even staged a bogus referendum to declare Uzbekistan's loyalty to the Soviet Union.

Only when it was completely clear that the USSR was defunct did Karimov declare Uzbekistan independent and himself to be the nationalist leader who had heroically led the new country to freedom. He quickly took full control of the property, security and governance apparatus of the former

Communist Party and continued to run independent Uzbekistan along Soviet lines, minus the fig leaf of ideology. He used the power this gave him to grab great personal wealth and has retained dictatorial control ever since.

All in all then, Tashkent did not sound like many peoples' idea of a plum posting. It was a small Embassy in a remote country that no-one had ever heard of, let alone considered important. Indeed, it made the backwater of Georgetown, Guyana that I had rejected a few years earlier sound like Washington, D.C. But, once again, like Bucharest and unlike Dubai, it felt right and I was happy to be going there, especially as the job I had been given was Third Secretary Political. This was the kind of serious, albeit microscopically junior, political relations job I had always wanted from my Foreign Office career. As well as being a role I could really immerse myself in, it forced me to grow-up and help some people who really needed support.

Both of my postings so far featured a darker side that had increasingly nagged at my conscience amid all of the largely self-indulgent fun I was having. In Dubai, it was the treatment of low-paid migrant workers. In Bucharest, it was the orphans.

Whether in bars, restaurants or nightclubs, the fun of a night out in Bucharest in the early 1990s would often end with an abrupt dose of heart-wrenching reality. On leaving the venue, we would be approached by a group of street kids. They were mostly boys in their early to mid-teens dressed in grubby rags seeking food or some small change to buy it. I never established definitively what happened to most of the girls, although there were sickening rumours about brothels. The street kids were remarkably polite given their circumstances. Some had the engaging kind of youthful cheek that comes from living on your wits at a distressingly young age. Others were quiet, gaunt and haunted-looking. The story of how they came to be in their desperate situation was the most horrific legacy of Ceausescu's rule.

In the aftermath of the revolution, a chain of chronically neglected and over-populated orphanages was discovered across the country. The media descended upon them and broadcast scenes that shocked the world. They were filled with thousands of chronically underfed, dirty, pale and shaven-headed children confined to their cots and rocking in distress.

The orphanages were a product of Ceauşescu's transition from run-of-the-mill dictator to full-blown megalomaniac during the last decade of his rule. He decided that the scale of his genius as a leader was inadequately matched by the size of Romania's population and that more people deserved the good fortune of living under his rule. Aggressive territorial expansion was precluded by the deadlocked Cold War geopolitics of the era. Even if it had not been, the poorly resourced Romanian army would have struggled to fight its way through a shower curtain, let alone the iron one.

Instead, Ceauşescu ignored the fact that Romania's existing inhabitants were already struggling to subsist on what his calamitous system allowed them to produce and sought to increase the domestic population. Contraception and abortion were banned, with stiff punishments for any women found to be disobeying. To enforce his writ, Ceauşescu set up an inspectorate to conduct invasive health checks on women of child-bearing age who were failing to meet their quotas for producing children. Inevitably, this policy led to an increase in dangerous backstreet abortions and an epidemic of female health problems. Equally, the reproductive reign of terror succeeded in increasing the birth rate and led to the next disaster for Romanian society.

The penury in which majority of the population were kept meant that many families were completely unable to support the extra children the state had forced them to produce. In response, the government hastily opened a kiddy gulag archipelago of poorly funded, inadequately equipped orphanages run by untrained and barely-paid staff. The original plan was for them to accommodate the surplus children during the week when their parents were at work and to allow them to return home at weekends. Tragically, the enforced child birth policy quickly caused the orphanages to become crammed to the rafters. This overcrowding, combined with the bureaucratic incompetence of the authorities, led to thousands of kids being shuffled from one orphanage to another and becoming irrevocably lost to their parents.

As if that was not tragic enough, the Ceauşescus managed to add a further twist of horror to the story. Elena, the President's wife, had long fancied herself as a scientist and had been festooned with eminent titles, despite her absolute lack of any genuine scientific aptitude. She hit upon the idea that periodically injecting an extra pint of blood into young bodies would cause them to grow into a super race – something she thought might prove useful in the forthcoming quest for global domination. Elena had little trouble in selling this idea to her husband and they decided that the orphans, now that they had been detached from their parents or any other authority figure who might be tempted to object, would be the ideal beneficiaries of their masterplan.

This scheme might have ended up as just one more of the litany of crackpot ideas perpetrated by the Ceauşescus and need not have ended quite so catastrophically. But their desire to keep their idea secret led them to source black market blood via their shady contacts in the global despots' network. The precise provider has never been confirmed but it was an equally poor and misruled country where the, as yet, little understood AIDS virus was taking hold. The net result was that a large number of the already malnourished and psychologically traumatised kids in the orphanages were infected with HIV as well.

Some of them who survived to be old enough to escape from or get kicked out of the orphanages were the ones who I met living in groups on the streets of Bucharest. They used to sleep in the sewers, where it was warmer and safe from the police and other abusers. They survived, barely, if at all, by scavenging in dustbins and, as I discovered, begging for food outside restaurants and bars. When they could not find anything to eat, some of the street children sniffed solvents to stave off the hunger.

The more enterprising among them would try to eke out a living by cleaning car windscreens at traffic lights, which was then a novelty and the first time I had seen anyone doing such a thing. In early 1990s Bucharest, it was a genuinely useful service because windscreen wipers, like most things, were hard to find in the shops and constantly being nicked if you forgot to take them off and carry them with you every time you parked. The problem was that the poor kids rarely had access to anything more than a filthy rag soaked in water from the drains.

Even allowing for the inadequacies of the service, I was always astonished at the small-minded attitude of some expatriates towards these street kids. They would get apoplectic at them for messing up the windscreens of their expensive cars and moan about how annoying it was when the kids were reluctant to take no for an answer. I regularly pointed out that this was minor irritation when compared with having to live in the sewers, eat from the bins and die young from AIDS, but it rarely seemed to mollify some of my compatriots.

I always kept a supply of clean wash leathers in the car to be handed out to the kids whenever they appeared at the traffic lights, which seemed like a better solution to me. This gave them the means to do a decent job and legitimately earn a crust. But I did not make many converts on that one either.

In hindsight, I was on shaky ground when it came to being harsh on others. The sum total of my help to the Romanian orphanages and street kids was one Saturday morning spent painting, a few small cash donations, some surplus food from restaurants, the wash leathers and appropriating a bit of cast-off Embassy furniture for them. All I did for the exploited workers in Dubai was to fulfill my official duty by refusing visas to those domestic staff who did not meet the requirements of the rules, probably making their employment position even worse in the process.

This was a pitiful contribution from someone who could preach about the injustice of it all for hours on end. My job in Tashkent would allow no such backsliding.

12. Fight for Your Rights

THE main part of my brief in Tashkent was dealing with human rights issues in what was a brutal police state and that meant there would be no pontificating from the side-lines this time. The role demanded a hands-on approach, a concept I was to apply all too literally by the end of my posting.

When I arrived there in 1996, I was delighted to discover that I would be living in a country that I had previously thought history had removed from my potential list of destinations: the Soviet Union. Despite five years of independence from the defunct USSR, Tashkent still looked like a Soviet city with its TV tower, rattling trolleybuses, drab shops, wide, half-empty boulevards and policemen in pizza-sized hats on every corner.

President Karimov had made a few cosmetic alterations to the city after independence. The vapid billboard slogans glorifying the nation were now accompanied by an Uzbek flag, rather than a hammer and sickle. And the statues of Karl Marx and Lenin were knocked off their plinths to be replaced by ones of Amir Timur, more commonly known in the West as Tamerlane, a harsh fourteenth century ruler who had rampaged across Central Asia and been adopted as the new national icon by Karimov, who relished the implicit comparison.

On more substantive matters, Karimov used the collapse of the USSR to turn the clock back to a time before the liberated Gorbachev era. His distance from deference to Moscow allowed him to establish a harsher regime than anything seen since Stalin's days. There was no freedom of speech, the media and the legal system were entirely directed by the government and tight state control was strangling the economy. Anyone who complained about the situation risked being imprisoned, tortured and killed.

The first people to discover the reality of Karimov's rule were the leaders and activists of the democratic political parties, such as Erk and Birlik, which appeared after independence. They mistakenly believed that the declaration of multi-party democracy in the new republic's constitution was serious. Karimov quickly disabused them of this notion and deployed the full powers of his police state to crush them. They were effectively prevented from functioning and their leaders were either jailed or, in the case of a lucky few, forced into exile.

Karimov's next targets were the small number of independent human rights organisations. Their aim was to persuade the government to adhere to the stipulations of international legislation, and the justice and democracy provisions in its own Constitution. These independent activists were mostly skint, eccentric and prone to quarrelling amongst themselves. They were also perhaps the bravest collection of people I have ever had the privilege to meet. It takes a phenomenal amount of courage to campaign on behalf of people who have been abducted, beaten, tortured and killed by the security forces, in the full knowledge that doing so puts you high on the list to be next.

Once they had been reduced to a small and essentially unthreatening size, the regime did sometimes use more subtle tactics than sheer brutality to keep them in line. One of the methods used to distract attention from them was to create a façade of lavishly-funded human rights organisations directed by the government. These were known with appropriate Orwellian absurdity as GONGOs – Government Organised Non-Governmental Organisations. The only indication I ever saw that Karimov possessed a sense of humour, albeit a dark one, was when he appointed the daughter of his disgraced predecessor, Sayara Rashidova, to head the most prominent of them. Their purpose was to engage in all manner of pointless activity, often organising endless talking-shop conferences, to hoodwink the outside world into believing that the Uzbek regime was serious about the issues while staying well clear of doing anything that might actually hinder Karimov from abusing his people at will. At least it indicated that the regime had a modicum of interest in how it was perceived by the outside world.

The human rights defenders were quick to spot this chink of light. One of the ways in which they sought to protect people was to work closely with the major international organisations such as Human Rights Watch, and interested foreign governments. Their hope was that we could exert some influence on the Uzbek regime or at least embarrass it into moderating its abuses by making clear that we were watching them.

It was my job in the Embassy to liaise with them, monitor and report to London on systemic abuses and lobby the Uzbek government about changing its behaviour. We worked closely together with our European Union and Organisation for Security and Cooperation in Europe (OSCE) colleagues because both were organisations with which the

Uzbek government wanted good relations. Such cooperation enabled us to share information and multiply our influence by producing joint reports, statements and recommendations for action against the Uzbek government.

As always with Embassy political relations jobs, my first task was to become well-informed about what was going on. That involved making contact with other diplomatic colleagues, particularly the Germans and Americans, who had the largest and most engaged Embassies in Tashkent at the time, the OSCE office and NGOs such as the Open Society Institute and the International Committee of the Red Cross. Even though I had been forewarned about the dire human rights situation in my briefings before travelling to Tashkent, I was horrified by what my colleagues told me.

Apart from the activists, thousands of ordinary people had been arrested by the security forces. Some of them had, for example, been overheard criticising the authorities by its omnipresent informers or seen attending an unofficial social or religious gathering. Others did not seem to have committed even those nebulous crimes. The detainees were then subjected to both physical and psychological torture. Methods commonly used included beatings, electric shocks, hanging by the wrists and ankles, rape and sexual humiliation, asphyxiation with plastic bags and gas masks, threats of physical harm to relatives, and denial of food or water. Often they were then given a show trial, followed by a long prison sentence accompanied by continued torture.

In addition to meeting my international colleagues, I also made first-hand contact with the Uzbek people suffering under the regime's reign of terror. The story they had to tell was even worse. Members of the public were often picked up when on routine errands such as popping to the shops and disappeared indefinitely, with the authorities denying the family any information about what had happened to their loved ones. For some families, the next time they saw their relative was when they were returned to them as a battered, barely recognisable corpse in a cheap plywood coffin. Others were never heard from again.

The region worst affected by the abuses was the Ferghana Valley. This fertile land is the most densely populated area of Uzbekistan but is separated from the rest of the country by the high Tien-Shan Mountains. Its geographical isolation has always encouraged an independent spirit. Ferghana was the heartland of the Basmachi rebels that the Soviets had initially struggled to subdue in the 1920s and slightly more of the pre-Soviet cultural and religious traditions had survived there than in other parts of the country. Karimov also received some challenging receptions on his visits to the Valley during the brief period after independence when freedom and democracy still seemed to be a possibility. He has harboured a vendetta against the people there ever since.

With the assistance of my contacts I made several discreet trips to the Ferghana Valley, neglecting to seek the official permission and dreary calls on local officials that the all-controlling Uzbek government obliged us to obtain. In towns such as Andizhan and Namangan and rural districts, I stayed with local people in their traditional houses. They invariably had no electricity or running water and had to rely on pit latrines and bucket showers in their back yards. Poverty was pervasive and several of the families I stayed with had essentially become detached from the cash economy. They survived by bartering goods, services and the food they produced with others in a similar position.

Despite their straitened circumstances, all of them were astonishingly warm and hospitable, including providing the best food and comfort they were able to offer their guest. It was clear our interest gave them a lift, although I often worried about inflating their expectations of my power to help them.

My hosts had some appalling stories to tell about fathers, sons and brothers who had been battered, jailed or disappeared without trace. Apart from the trauma caused by such suffering, families that had been robbed of their main bread-winner also faced immense practical difficulties of day-to-day survival because there was no social security system to fall back on. There were streets in some of the major towns where roughly every second family home was missing someone at the hands of the regime. Many of the relatives spoke, convincingly, of their bafflement as to why their loved one had been taken because they had not been involved in politics or illicit religious activities.

Now that the political opposition had been crushed, religion was probably of greatest concern to the regime. Mosques and other places of worship were potentially the only remaining places where people might gather in large groups to discuss ideas and the state of affairs in the country. As a consequence, the government cracked down hard on any semblance of religious freedom. They created a network of state-controlled mosques, with the Imams' Friday sermon being scripted and distributed nationwide by the central authorities in Tashkent.

Such repression was worse than the later Soviet decades, when some mild freedom of religion had been tolerated, especially in places like Ferghana where it was deeply rooted in the social fabric. One of my regular contacts was the son of prominent, moderate but independent Imam who was brazenly taken away by the security police whilst waiting to board a flight at Tashkent airport to attend an international conference. He was never seen again.

My trips around the country seemed to confirm what the victims' families had told me - that it was not even necessary to commit a mild act of disobedience such as attending a non-state sanctioned religious service, in order to be arrested. The authorities were intent on creating a climate of fear by not even bothering to restrict their abuses to those who did not toe the government line. In that they had succeeded and many people were living in terror of a knock at their door or of not returning whenever they went out.

One concession the authorities did make to diplomats was to allow us to attend the show trials of some of the detainees. This was a commitment they had made in various international forums but I have no idea why they did. They cannot have believed that we would be won over by seeing their version of due process in action for ourselves. It was obvious that there was no independent rule of law in Uzbekistan and the trials were a complete travesty that only provided further proof of the malevolent nature of the government.

The defendants were kept in a small cage in the courtroom and often betrayed signs of mistreatment. They were rarely allowed to speak other than to confirm the seemingly spurious confessions that had been tortured out of them in custody or fabricated by the security forces. Rather than political activism which, theoretically, was legal under Uzbek law, the charges were almost always identical ones of possession of drugs. These were apparently routinely planted on the defendants by the arresting officers. The practice reached such ridiculous proportions that it became common for Uzbek men in some areas to cut the pockets out of their clothes. Unfortunately this ruse proved short-lived because the security services soon stopped going through the motions of supposedly planting evidence and started appearing to lie to the courts that the drugs had been found in the defendants' possession. The state-appointed defence lawyer, who had usually been denied access to his clients, rarely intervened in court other than to make a brief, ritual plea for leniency. And the judges, who were responsible for the verdict in what was a non-jury system, often berated the defendants about their heinous crimes whilst the superficial process of establishing their guilt or innocence was still in progress. Unsurprisingly, no defendant was ever found not guilty because the sentence had, to all intents, been decreed in advance to the judge by the government.

It soon became clear to me that retaining some diplomatic detachment in these circumstances was going to be difficult and, frankly, I did not try too hard. Unlike many issues in international relations and diplomatic life, there was no grey area here between right and wrong. I quickly realised that my main role was to drum up whatever pressure I could on the Uzbek government to change its ways.

At the time, human rights protection was high on the global agenda. Partly this was a product of the free world's shame at its failure to prevent the massacres in Bosnia and Rwanda earlier in the decade. There was also a looser sense that the euphoria unleashed by the fall of communism and hoped for rise of democracy was going awry in much of the former Soviet Union. The feeling was that the Cold War could not be said to have been won if communist dictators were merely replaced by ideology-free despots, especially if they were one and the same person, as in Uzbekistan.

In keeping with this atmosphere, a new Labour government had come to power shortly before my arrival in Tashkent, and its Foreign Secretary, Robin Cook, had announced that our foreign policy would henceforth have, 'an ethical dimension,' with, 'human rights at the heart of it'.

Apart from it being my job to implement government policy, I believed strongly in the ideals of human rights. They are not some abstract, high-minded political concept but the essential conditions for being able to live a decent life. Without them, there is no free speech in public discussions or private debates, you cannot travel when or where you wish, choose what you read, watch or listen to because the media, books and internet are strictly controlled by the state, which only permits access to the information it wants you to see. Personal property or businesses can be seized or shut-down by corrupt officials with no possibility for legal redress. Your children may also suffer. In the example of Uzbekistan, school kids are removed from their classrooms for several weeks each year to perform unpaid, backbreaking work harvesting the cotton crop and their parents can do nothing about it.

In addition to the powerful moral arguments, there are hard-headed pragmatic reasons for working to support human rights in other countries. Democracies that respect the rights of their people seldom end up going to war with each other. Free countries tend to be better long-term trading partners too, as, even allowing for the current global economic crisis, they are more enduringly prosperous and inhibit official corruption. Uzbekistan was a case in point. There was no chance of the UK doing much business in the country and it was a source of security threats to us.

The intense oppression practiced in such places causes radicalisation. The Uzbek regime's bogus refrain was that they would love to institute democracy but could not do so because their opponents were all extremist Islamist terrorists who freedom would allow to take over the country, so they had to be crushed first. It is true that there were actually some small groups of violent Islamist radicals lurking in and around Uzbekistan, such as the Islamic

Movement of Uzbekistan (IMU). But there was no sign that such groups had any more than a few hundred active members or much popular support. In contrast to the official Uzbek line, I always found that the widespread refusal by the Uzbek people to fall for simplistic, extremist ideas was a remarkable testimony to their moderation.

Such moderation could not last forever though. The Uzbek government, by behaving so viciously and corruptly, denying any hope of a better life to its people and closing down dissent was ultimately creating fertile ground for the extremists to recruit from. Their numbers steadily increased during the time I was there. The militants also became bolder, launching a terrifying series of bombings and armed attacks in Tashkent during the late 1990's.

Western democracies discovered the direct danger the extremists presented a few years later when the IMU fought alongside Al-Qaeda in Afghanistan. These national security concerns should have added to the already strong moral case for pressurising the Uzbek government into ending its human rights abuses. It is regrettable, then, that British governments in later years, after 9/11, sometimes deviated from this policy and fell for the Karimov regime's line about being a bulwark against Islamist extremism, rather than a cause of it.

On a personal level, I often wondered how I would react if I was a young man living under such brutal repression with no prospects and absolutely no peaceful avenues for complaint while the authorities abducted, tortured and killed my closest family members. I might not have needed much persuasion to grow a beard, grab a gun and head up to join the guerrillas in the mountains to do something about it. Even as a cossetted foreign diplomat, two and a half years of meeting relatives of the tortured and disappeared and seeing contacts and friends being beaten or imprisoned was starting to become too much.

One morning I went to observe a protest by forty or so mothers, wives and sisters of disappeared menfolk outside Tashkent City Hall. When I arrived, I found the women, who had gone there to request a meeting with the mayor to inform him about their cases, being jostled and filmed by the security police, who liked to use the recordings to threaten people in later interrogations.

I found it impossible to stand idly by and ended up getting in-between one particularly frail and frightened looking old lady and the security policeman who was manhandling her whilst pushing his big, heavy, old-style video camera into her face. I shoved him firmly away from the woman, sending him staggering backwards and the camera clattering into his face. Simultaneously, I put on my gruffest Hull accent to ask him, amongst other less polite comments, if beating up grannies for a living made him feel like a hard man. The security thug was unused to anyone being unhinged enough to fight back and retreated in confusion to join his colleagues. Thankfully, they were also non-plussed and decided to take matters no further.

My only inner regret was that I had failed to knock his lights out completely. Even on reflection, I cannot say that I think what I did was wrong on a human level. But, apart from getting some anger out of my system and cheering up the protesting women by providing some unexpectedly hands-on support, it did not help anyone much either. Indeed, acting in such a way might have increased the risk of later reprisals. In any case, it was certainly not appropriate conduct for a diplomat and I realised that, by ditching my detached perspective, I had outlived my usefulness in Uzbekistan.

13. Silken Happiness

AWAY from the emotional intensity of work, everyday life in Uzbekistan was often surprisingly pleasant and a lot of fun. The weather was great for a start – over 300 days of sunshine per year, ranging from baking dry heat in the summer to beautifully crisp bright days in the winter. I always enjoyed the drive to work too, heading towards the view of the pristine snow-capped mountains in the distance above the concrete cityscape.

My house, in a traditional Uzbek 'mahalla' or neighbourhood, was built by my landlord. His attempt to create a traditional Swiss-style wooden chalet had turned out more of a garden shed on steroids. The house had several eccentricities such as the bathroom being tacked on to the kitchen for reasons of plumbing convenience. But it was comfortable and featured a mirrored ceiling in the kitchen and a nice, fully enclosed courtyard with a diesel generator in the corner.

The generator was a godsend during the frequent power cuts in Tashkent. The catch was that it sounded like a Spitfire revving up in the back garden. But at least it provided enough electricity to enable you to watch the telly while the noise it was making kept you awake. I loved watching

Hollywood films on Uzbek state TV. Dire warnings would flash up on screen periodically informing you that you were illegally watching a pirated video and should call the FBI immediately. And the dubbing of all of the roles, male and female, was done by a single, bass-voiced man, adding a compelling comic dimension to the direst romantic comedy.

My favourite thing about the house, though, was that one of the neighbours ran a small, clay oven bakery from his backyard that made fantastic Uzbek lipyoshka bread. Sometimes the simple pleasures are the greatest – smelling it as it came out of the oven and juggling it back down the street because it was too hot to hold was pure joy.

Uzbekistan is also home to several stunning ancient Silk Road cities, such as Samarkand, Bukhara and Khiva. In all of my posts there has always been one attraction that I have found astounding on my first visit, still loved on the second but felt sick of the sight of this place by the time I accompanied my umpteenth visitor there. In Uzbekistan, it was Samarkand. At first acquaintance, standing amid the magnificent blue-tiled buildings of its Registan Square felt like an *Arabian Nights* fantasy. By the end of my time in Uzbekistan, it was barely more evocative than an afternoon in the bathroom decorations department of B&Q.

Perhaps because I went there less, Bukhara was my favourite. They are all magnificent in their own way but it had less of an open air museum atmosphere and truly felt like an ancient city where everyday life was continuing much as it had done for centuries. Even more than most places in Uzbekistan, the people tended to wear their colourful traditional clothing, such as the chapan robe – an ornately embroidered outer garment that resembles a cross between a long coat and a dressing gown – and tubeteyka caps, while going about their daily business.

The authentic feeling was enhanced by staying in one of the small bed and breakfast hotels that had sprung up in the old houses in the heart of the city, despite the government's heavy-handed restrictions on private enterprise, and eating at a chaikhana, a traditional Uzbek teahouse. These delightful establishments are often open air, with a canopy for shade, comfy bed-sized seats and an eternal role as the social centre of local life.

The most popular dishes throughout Uzbekistan are shashlik, a grilled meat kebab, and plov, a type of fried rice with vegetables and mutton. Both are usually delicious but plov, in particular, is often the source of some wry amusement. Everywhere you go, the locals will tell you that their unique recipe is better than that of any other town or region. But two and a half years and several hundred servings was not sufficient to grasp the subtleties because they all tasted exactly the same to me, from one end of the country to the other.

Often it was possible to combine a work trip with some Silk Road tourism. In fact, this was a good idea because it provided cover for what were sometimes semi-clandestine meetings with activists and victims' families, in an attempt to avoid drawing more unwanted attention onto them from the Uzbek authorities.

One of my favourite places to visit was Urgench, a modern city next-door to Khiva, because there was, almost uniquely in Uzbekistan, a small, independent, local TV station there run by two brothers. They were very smart, sparky operators who we occasionally helped by providing some programming from the UK. They had set up their station as a commercial enterprise but also used it subtly to draw attention to the corruption and incompetence of the authorities.

Their favourite technique was to use minor local news stories to make oblique points that their savvier viewers would not miss. An example during one of my visits was a report about a child falling into a drainage ditch. An interview with the child's parents was followed by the local mayor innocently being asked why a fence around the ditch had never been built, even though money had been allocated for it in the last council budget. The item then closed with footage of the mayor climbing into his gleaming Mercedes and driving off at speed – thus providing a clear visual answer to the question he had failed to respond to in words. Eventually, though, the authorities cottoned on to this subtlety, closed down the station and the brothers fled the country before a worse fate befell them.

One of the less pleasant aspects of going to places like Urgench was that you had to fly to get there. I am not a happy flyer which is another reason why the Diplomatic Service was an unlikely choice of career. But, far from being a phobia, the state of repair of many of Uzbek Airlines' antique planes made it genuinely dangerous.

On one trip back from Urgench, my nerves were not being helped by sitting sweating for over an hour on the tarmac in a packed, unventilated rust-bucket of a plane. The flowery kitchen floor linoleum that had been used to decorate the cabin several decades earlier was melting in the 100 degree plus heat. I tried to distract myself by reading a ten day old copy of *The Independent* that had come through the diplomatic bag. We still had not moved when I finished the paper and the two scruffy, gold-toothed and less than fragrant Uzbek peasants sitting next to me began asking for it. I confirmed irritably, that they did not speak English and haughtily pointed out to them that they would not be able to read it. They apparently did not understand much Russian either because they continued politely requesting the paper. Eventually, I relented and gave it to them with a final petulant comment about the incomprehensible English text. The man next to me took the newspaper with a gracious smile, calmly ripped it into halves, folded them neatly and gave one to his friend. The pair then began fanning themselves to cool off. Sometimes even the most down-to-earth diplomat needs bringing down a peg or two.

My co-passenger that day was greatly amused by my humbling which was understandable because she is the reason why Uzbekistan, despite its difficulties, will always remain special to me. It was the place where I met my African Queen - the love of my life and future wife who I married after we had moved on together to Brussels.

Our paths first crossed when I was having dinner with friends one evening in a hotel restaurant. We had just ordered when a sweating vision in a baggy tracksuit, known to one of the others at the table, flowed elegantly in from the gym and joined us. I remember being struck by the thought that if she could make such an impact on me in that state then she really must be something special when she was scrubbed up. The circumstances of that evening made it awkward for me to ask her for an opportunity to confirm my first impressions. But I did make a careful note of who she was with a view to following-up and the social circuit in Tashkent was small enough to ensure that we had a couple of other subsequent chance encounters soon afterwards.

The first of them came at a house party thrown by an American diplomatic colleague and ended inauspiciously. I was delighted to find her among the partygoers and to see from across the courtyard that my initial assessment had, in fact, massively underestimated her beauty. On chatting to her, I was even more thrilled to discover that she had a striking personality that oozed wit, warmth and charisma. In case all of that was not already impressive enough, I also found out that she was a hyper-intelligent Harvard graduate of Kenyan-Italian extraction who had learnt to speak fluent Russian for fun and, as a result, ended-up obtaining a senior job with an American law firm in Tashkent at an unusually young age. Given this overload of enticing qualities, it might not, then, have been the smartest move on my part to allow her to escape by turning down flat her offer to dance.

To someone like my wife, for whom dancing is a natural expression of joy, this must have seemed cold and odd. But for someone as useless on the dance-floor as me, it was an essential defensive strategy to avoid ruining my chances by making a fool of myself before I had even started. Fortunately, in a contrary way, my refusal helped by confirming to her that I was so obviously miles away from her idea of boyfriend material that it would be safe to go out with me a couple of times just for some platonic company.

In this regard, I have to be grateful to Uzbekistan for having so few social outlets and being a place where the competition from the menfolk, both local and expatriate, was so feeble. As my wife is occasionally fond of reminding me, if we had met anywhere else then I might never have been given the opportunity to convince her of my appeal before she even realised what was happening.

Not only that, she provided the ultimate cure for my more dangerous, booze-fuelled, tendencies.

14. Abdullojonov the Car Salesman

APART from covering Uzbekistan, our tiny embassy in Tashkent was also accredited to another obscure former Soviet republic next door, Tajikistan. It was a fascinating place with predominantly Persian cultural roots rather than the Turkic ones of the other Central Asian states. It also had charming, hospitable people and staggering natural beauty. But a nasty civil war and the lack of significant British interests in the country meant that we had not opened an embassy there when it became independent.

There was, though, just enough going on politically to warrant keeping some sort of British government eye on Tajikistan. As a global trading nation and still significant international player, we try not to have any black holes in our knowledge anywhere, and I was given responsibility for covering it from Tashkent instead. This was an intriguing but tricky role because we were forbidden from travelling to Tajikistan by the Foreign Office's Security Department for the same reasons why we did not have a resident embassy in the first place.

At first I was tempted to argue with their instructions as the war was mostly confined to certain regions and, if it had been up to me, would not have stopped me from visiting. My views changed, though, when I heard that the only realistic way to get to the capital, Dushanbe, was in a tiny, ancient Yak-40 propeller plane over the colossal Tien Shan mountain range. Suddenly I lost all sense of urgency and settled for monitoring it from a safe distance.

The civil war there was ostensibly between Islamist rebels and a secular clan of former communist officials. In practice, it often seemed to be a messy squabble between various regional, factional and criminal interests for control of the few assets the country possessed. These included the transit traffic in heroin from Afghanistan next door, an aluminium smelter, a few mines and precious little else.

Putting together any information on what was going on in Tajikistan involved monitoring the country's press, a regular cuppa at the Tajik Embassy in Tashkent, talking to the few foreigners who were based there - mostly a handful of UN workers and the German Embassy - and collaring any source I could who had actually been to the country.

My friend, Joe Sherry, was one of the first people I approached because he had previously worked as a manager at one of the mines. Unfortunately, Joe was not very informative, as he had hardly ever left the remote complex due to the precarious security situation in the area. Perhaps the only thing I picked up from him was an insight into the modest resources available to the Tajik army. He told me how the mine, as an important strategic national asset, had been given an emergency hotline to contact should rebel forces ever attempt to take it over. One day this came to pass and Joe duly did as bided before retreating under his bed in the accommodation block. From there he listened for about an hour to heavy gunfire rattling all around the mine. It was finally followed by a few minutes silence and a firm knock at the door.

After a few moments of misgivings, Joe decided that he had little option but to accept his visitor's loud assertions that he was the commanding officer of the Tajik Army Special Forces. He opened the top half of the stable-style door and was pleasantly surprised to see a very professional looking soldier dressed in an immaculate combat jacket and helmet and carrying a modern machine gun. The officer explained that the rebels had been chased away but that he needed to inspect all of the buildings to make sure none were still lurking around. Relieved, Joe opened the bottom half of the door to let him in, whereupon he saw that the rest of the officer's uniform consisted of a pair of pyjama bottoms and flip-flops.

For all of its destructive nastiness, the Tajik civil war did feature some colourful characters that made it undeniably interesting to follow. Most of the various rebel commanders were known by nicknames such as Ali the Boxer and, my personal favourite, Rizvon Hitler. I was intrigued to read a Russian press interview with Mr Hitler one day in which he explained that his nom-de-guerre was not, as widely assumed, an attempt to instil terror into his enemies. The nickname was in fact one he had been stuck with since childhood. Apparently, he had been chosen to play the Nazi dictator in his village primary school play about how the heroic Soviets had defeated the fascists in World War II and given a memorable performance in the role. Much to his ongoing annoyance, everyone in his home region had called him Hitler ever since.

We did occasionally manage to make direct contact with some prominent Tajiks when they were in Tashkent. One such figure was a former Prime Minister, Abdumalik Abdullojonov. He had been deposed in 1994 and had recently launched a failed armed assault on Dushanbe in an attempt to seize power from the President, Emomali Rakhmonov. Mr Abdullojonov had a fearsome reputation and we made contact with him via the car dealership he was now running in Tashkent. Somewhat to my surprise, he agreed to come around to the Embassy one summer afternoon to meet me and the Ambassador over tea and sandwiches in the garden.

Mr Abdullojonov rolled up to the Embassy gates in a massive white limousine that would have stood out on the streets of Las Vegas, let alone among the ubiquitous Daewoo's of Tashkent. I was daunted to see a huge bloke emerge from the limousine looking like the manager of a World Wrestling Federation baddies tag team. One of the many allegations against Mr Abdullojonov was a massive fraud involving the Tajik cotton harvest. He was certainly wearing a significant proportion of it in the form of a dazzling, Cadillac-matching white suit, shoes and hat, accessorised with some spectacular gold jewellery. Despite having dressed the part of a dapper don, Mr Abdullojonov denied all knowledge of his alleged gangsterism and coup-mongering. But he was engaging company and our chat with him was one of the more intriguingly odd but agreeable hours I spent at work in Tashkent. I do not recall picking up too much about Tajik politics but, as the son of a used car dealer, we had an instant affinity and I was gratified to learn that the business attracts similar characters from Hull to the Himalayas.

The war finally began to calm down towards the end of my posting and I belatedly obtained permission from the Foreign Office to test the waters with a visit to the northern Leninabad province, which was drivable from Tashkent and isolated from the rest of the country by the mountains.

On arrival in Khojand, the dusty and dilapidated provincial capital, the Embassy driver, Ghaffour and I, were met by a local city official and taken to its one functioning hotel, where we had booked rooms. As I stood at the front desk checking-in, I sensed that something was amiss when the previously welcoming receptionist turned pale and suddenly began to tell me that the hotel was full after all. I began to complain but soon stopped after following the receptionist's gaze over my shoulder to see half-a-dozen machine gun toting bruisers coming up the steps from a fleet of black Mercedes with tinted windows. The gentlemen concerned crashed into the reception area and announced brusquely that they would be taking all of the rooms with immediate effect. Credit cards were unheard of at that time in Khojand but their AK-47s proved sufficient to guarantee their reservation.

I did not really need the advice by this point but our local escort quickly suggested that we seek alternative accommodation and we scarpered as quickly and unobtrusively as possible. As we drove away, he told me that the hotel's unexpected guests were a notorious warlord cum drug boss and his men, whom it was generally best not to argue with. Clearly Tajikistan was not yet quite as secure as hoped.

Visitors to Khojand had been scarce over recent years, so finding somewhere to stay was now a problem. After a couple of hours of searching for permission and a key, our friend from the council eventually got us in to an old guesthouse that had formerly been used by visiting communist party officials from around the Soviet Union. Unfortunately, no-one had stayed there since the USSR had collapsed eight years earlier. Half of the windows were broken, everything was covered in thick dust and there was no running water to wash the cobwebs out of the bath. On the plus side it had a great view of the river and the huge statue of Lenin that still overlooked the city. The rest of the visit passed peacefully but somehow I never quite managed to get back to Tajikistan again.

15. Get on the Bus

UNLIKE my previous posting, some of the fun in Uzbekistan was provided by my compatriots because Tashkent featured a preponderance of ex-pats with good reasons for not going back home.

Tashkent was an oddball outpost. Very few of the large UK-based companies that had set-up there during the optimistic early post-independence years were still present by 1996. Those that had maintained a reduced presence were doing so mainly because they had invested too much to give up and bail-out, rather than out of any real optimism that the business climate would improve.

One of their biggest problems was that the Uzbek currency, the Sum, could not be freely converted on the exchange markets into money that had any value outside of Uzbekistan. Companies relied on the Uzbek government to exchange their earnings for hard cash, which, despite repeated promises, they rarely did. A side effect of the unattractive investment climate was that, aside from the handful of run-of-the-mill executives from the big companies that were clinging on, the small British community consisted mostly of mysterious traders, gold miners and assorted duckers and divers whose actual commercial activities were hard to pin down.

Almost all of these desperados were male and either single or unaccompanied by their families due to the perception that it was too difficult a place for them to live. There was some truth in this but rather, the suspicion was that quite a few of these gentlemen found family-free life in Tashkent conducive to enjoying a second youth.

The cost of living what passed for the high life was rock-bottom. Most were paid in US dollars and the government's perverse economic policies meant that there was a flourishing black market offering currency exchange at anywhere between four and seven times the official rate. The only people in the entire country with access to dollars who were not able to take advantage of this situation were the four employees of the British Embassy. We were expressly banned from doing so by the Foreign Office Finance Department, which was the cause of some resentment on our part. Even all of our diplomatic colleagues from other embassies were benefitting. Instead of saving money as was the accepted norm when on hardship postings, we were blowing the bulk of our wages by being forced to pay prices that were, in effect, higher than Switzerland.

Some of the demand for hard currency came from small traders who travelled to China, Turkey and Dubai and came back laden with goods to sell on their market stalls. One of the ways they obtained their dollars was to post a female family member - the theory being that they were less likely than men to be beaten-up by the police during their frequent bribe-hunting raids - next to the small street that ran alongside the giant Alaski Bazaar food market. The women would wait there with carrier bags full of brick-sized wads of Uzbek Sum in cash, a common practice as the largest denomination of note was restricted to 100 Sum as a strategy to prevent inflation. The customers would then crawl slowly along the kerb in their cars, pausing to furtively roll down their windows and ask the ladies the going rate. There would then be a quick nod of agreement and the woman would swiftly scoop up the $100 note placed on the passenger seat and dump one of her plastic bags full of bundles of Sum in its place. All in all, it was a mightily efficient system and one I did not see replicated until I came across drive-by cashpoints of a more conventional nature in the USA a decade later.

The black market exchange rate meant that the ex-pat males were able to splash the cash even more extravagantly in the handful of bars and nightclubs in Tashkent. This did them no harm at all with the numerous mostly young and attractive local women who frequented these establishments and were seeking a route out of Uzbekistan. The women could hardly be blamed for this, especially the ethnic Russians and other Soviet nationalities who had been marooned there after the USSR sank. Some of them were a bit brazen.

I have it on good authority that these local ladies had a clear hierarchy of foreign catches. Americans were the rare blue-fin tuna at the top of the list as they were considered more attentive to their girlfriends' wishes as well as being able, of course, to get you all the way Stateside. The Brits came next because they were deemed, like haddock, to be solid and reliable – an assessment that was somewhat wide of the mark in the case of most of the ones I knew there. Other Europeans trailed in behind, fulfilling the cod role of being satisfactory if that was what was available. Various failings were attributed to them – the Germans were said to be too tight with their money, the Italians more interested in the woman looking after them than vice-versa and the French nowhere near as romantic as they were cracked up to be.

Some of the more genuine relationships that sprang from these unusual circumstances seemed set for success. One friend of mine married his Tatar girlfriend shortly before returning to the UK at the end of his contract in Uzbekistan. She convinced him that he must respect Tatar traditions by coming to seize her from her family home on horseback before the wedding ceremony. The nervous groom sourced a horse without too much difficulty. But Tashkent was hardly the wide-open Steppe land of Tatar lore and he fretted endlessly about how he was going to get the nag up to her twelfth floor flat in the tiny lift. The dilemma was still extant by the day of the wedding, as we stood suited and booted beneath the tower block with the shabby steed, debating whether it would be acceptable for him to carry her down over his shoulder instead. The matter was resolved when the bride suddenly swept past and around the corner into a waiting white Volga limousine, ruining her make-up with tears of laughter as she went. Her sense of humour was clearly destined to thrive in the UK.

It was harder to see where some of the other relationships were going. Tashkent was so far away from home that some married Western men treated it as a parallel universe. That quite a few of them would eagerly play the field available to them was predictable, if morally dubious. But others, such as Jim Shaughnessy, took it in a different direction entirely. Jim was a middle-aged bloke with a wife of long-standing and two kids back home in Ireland. Rather than seizing the second opportunity to sow his wild oats as many of his contemporaries did, he set up an entire duplicate married life of dull domestication with a demure young lady, complete with matching sweaters, dressing gowns and slippers ordered from the small ads pages of the *Daily Express*.

An ageing salt, Tommy Grey, declared himself too old for that kind of carry on. He was one of those endearingly eccentric characters that washed up regularly in Tashkent. My Embassy colleagues and I never quite figured out how – Tommy presented himself as the representative of a different British company every week, but never one that had any known business in Uzbekistan. He was astonishingly similar in appearance and character to Uncle Albert from *Only Fools and Horses*. No conversation with him, about any subject, was possible without him working in at least two shipwreck stories from his years at sea.

What Tommy did like to do was drink. He could be found supping away and dispensing yarns at any hour of the night at his corner bar stool in the notorious Zafar club. It was a rather racy establishment for Tashkent, although tame by global standards. It featured a large room with young women gyrating on stage in their underwear who would also sit on the customers' knees in-between turns. The greater attraction for Tommy, and I have to admit, me, was the cheap open-all-hours bar in the small room next door. Late one Saturday evening I found him in there looking like his beard was collapsing into his face. He glumly and gummily confessed to me that he had broken his usual rule by wandering into the main room the night before, succumbed to temptation and gone home with one of the girls. At some point during their night manoeuvres, Tommy's false teeth had gone missing in action and were never seen again.

Some of our other ex-pats had nocturnal adventures that I would have preferred not to hear about at all. One chore for a diplomat overseas is taking your turn as the duty officer. This involves being on call twenty four hours a day for a week in case of urgent out-of-hours requests from London or dire emergency calls from British citizens in distress, for example, as victims of crime, serious accidents or illness.

Once, on my watch, I was awoken from a deep sleep in the early hours of the morning by a deeply distressed British citizen who had met a young woman in a nightclub and taken her home. He lived in an apartment in a secure compound and the guards were refusing to let her into the building because she did not have the appropriate ID or permission to enter. Consequently, he called the duty officer to demand that his Embassy do something to help. When I was posted in Moscow, our Defence Section, staffed by blunt military officers, rather than eloquent Foreign Office types, had a sign on their door which read, 'Diplomacy is the art of telling someone to go to hell in a way that makes them look forward to the journey'. On this occasion, I came up with an elegant form of words advising the caller to perform the act he had in mind on himself and hung up the phone.

Such minor irritations did little to diminish the generally enjoyable social life I had in Uzbekistan. But, as with work, there was a distinct moment of clarity when I realised that I had been living in distant Central Asia for too long. My brother, Tony, who was visiting at the time, recalls sitting in a city centre bar with my friends and I one Saturday tea time after our customary weekend football game. As was the norm, an attractive young woman appeared on the small stage at one end of the bar to begin swinging around a steel pole. She was rudely ignored by our group as we pressed against the front window to ogle an even more striking attraction that had stopped in the street outside.

It was a curvy, brand new, state-of-the-art bus with glossy paintwork, sleek chrome wheels and tinted windows revealing a tantalising glimpse of the flickering video screens within. Compared to the usual battered, lurching, black smoke-belching trolleybuses of Tashkent, it looked like a vessel from outer space. Tony sat open-mouthed, unsure whether to be more stunned by the young lady in her undies or the bunch of Robinson Crusoes drooling over the first roadworthy bus they had seen in years. And it dawned on me that it might be time to find some transport out of Central Asia sharpish.

16. Ukraine: A Brief Appendix

THE normal Foreign Office postings routine was two stints overseas followed by one at home. Despite squeezing three overseas tours in Romania, the UAE and Uzbekistan out of Personnel, I was still unenthused about going back to London when another offer arrived a few days before my departure date from Tashkent. A colleague had pulled out of a posting to Ukraine and the Office needed a Russian speaker with experience of political work to go there urgently. Rather than return to London, I jumped at the chance to spend a year in another supposedly grim former Soviet country instead.

The offer of a posting to Kiev was attractive because it would be on temporary promotion as Second Secretary Political, Press and Public Affairs. Temporary promotions usually end up being made permanent, barring a major cock-up. And the size of the Embassy meant that I would, in effect, be a one-man political section in a strategically significant country that was at a crucial stage in its transition from communism to democracy. Ukraine turned out to be a much nicer place than its advance publicity had suggested too. I warmed to it to such an extent that I left piece of myself there forever; my appendix.

One day, about six months into my posting, I had severe abdominal pains and twice dragged myself across town to the Embassy's in-house doctor who dismissed them as a minor stomach bug, despite the absence of the usual symptoms. Later that evening, the pain became worse and I called a local out-of-hours emergency medical service instead. Their doctor took one look at me, had a brief feel of my abdomen and half-carried, half-dragged me down the four flights of stairs from my flat and into an ambulance. We then drove at high-speed, lights and sirens blaring to the clinic. All I can remember about the ride is wondering why the doctors looked so horrified about something so minor and were so keen to stop me from falling asleep on the way.

The reason was revealed when I woke up the next morning. The surgeon told me that I had arrived barely conscious with an appendix that had turned septic and burst. It was, he said calmly, one of the worst messes of its kind that he had ever seen and had taken several hours to clean up. By his reckoning, if I had got to the clinic even a few minutes later, my life could have been ended by a routine, easily detectable ailment that our negligent medic should have spotted earlier in the day. The surgeon said the decisive action taken by the medic, Valery Brichevskiy, who had responded to my call-out had been crucial and I was effusive in expressing my gratitude to him when I got the chance.

I had further reason to worry for my continued existence later in the day. As I settled down to enjoy some Ukrainian daytime TV, another bloke about the same age as me was wheeled in to share the room. Rather more excitingly, his abdominal complaint was the result of several pieces of lead being fired into it at high velocity during what he called a business discussion. After a brief, polite chat to compare injuries, he began making increasingly frantic phone calls imploring someone to collect him from the clinic before his adversaries got there to finish the job. The dubbed Brazilian soap operas on the TV suddenly seemed to lose their melodrama as my room-mate and I willed his associates to get there first. Mercifully, they eventually did and the bloke staggered off remarkably swiftly for someone who had just had four bullets removed from his stomach and a drip sticking out of his sharp suit.

Back at work, the West was making a concerted effort to support the democratic development of Ukraine in opposition to the malign influence of Russia on it. Some liberal Ukrainians, and the nationalists from the West of the country, saw joining NATO and the EU as the best way to secure their nation's independence from the ogre to the East. Others were less sure, unsurprisingly given decades of Cold War era Soviet propaganda about NATO and the West's malevolent intentions. This sentiment was at its most pronounced in the more-Sovietised, Russian-speaking East of the country, closer to the border. To reassure these sceptical Ukrainians, we NATO member state Embassies had launched a programme of outreach activities to show them that what was being offered to them was cooperation and security.

And so it was that I found myself boarding a Ukrainian Air Force plane one freezing morning in Kiev, with a small group of Ambassadors from NATO HQ in Brussels. These included the German Ambassador, von Moltke, a descendent of the Prussian Generals of that name who had played prominent roles in Teutonic history and led the country's forces in World War I. We had arranged several speaking engagements for the Ambassadors in Donetsk, via a brief stopover in Dnipropetrovsk.

I had been rather nervous about boarding such a plane in the midst of an icy and snowy winter. In the days running up to the trip, I recalled all of the worst flights I have ever endured, one of which was from Istanbul to Tashkent a few months earlier. In that instance, the plane had been making some awful grinding noises for about half-an-hour after take-off which prompted the pilot to return to Istanbul for repairs. When we eventually got air-bound again, the pilot thought it a good idea to go around the cabin reassuring the passengers that all was well. Personally, I would have been more comforted to know that he was up front flying his patched-up plane, rather than wandering around at the back chatting.

With that experience in mind, the trip on the Ukrainian military transporter turned out to be one of the least nerve-wracking flights of my life. It was much smaller and older than the passenger airliner but I found it greatly reassuring to see the crew through the open cockpit door constantly checking dials, flicking switches and generally given the impression of being totally focused on what they were doing.

It probably helped too that the plane was normally used by Ukrainian generals and was laid out like a studio flat, rather than a cramped, conventional aircraft. There were sofas and a fridge in the corner. The military maps on the walls and my fertile imagination made it feel like we were preparing a secret World War II mission behind enemy lines and I contentedly contemplated growing a handlebar moustache. We also flew at such a low altitude that I was confident I could bail out at any time without risking anything more than a broken ankle.

The stopover to drop a couple of the Ambassadors off in Dnipropetrovsk sparked one of those dream-like moments I sometimes experienced in the Foreign Office when time stood still and I wondered how on earth I had got there. We landed on a snowy military base and disembarked for about half an hour onto the tarmac. All around were MiG fighter jets, some of them deafeningly taking off and landing on training flights just a few metres away, as military men in Soviet-style uniforms and big fur hats strode purposefully around. It all felt a very long way away from Hull Docks.

I had an even more pronounced bout of the James Bonds during a later trip to the same city as part of the same programme. This time I was accompanying a delegation from the Royal United Services Institutes (RUSI), the preeminent think-tank in the UK on defence and security issues. The programme we had organised for them included a rare visit to the Pivdenmash missile factory. This vast complex had produced the Soviet Union's first atomic missiles and a large part of its subsequent nuclear arsenal. For much of its history, the top secret plant had been disguised as a factory for producing agricultural machinery and strictly closed to outsiders. Rows of rusting tractors were still standing in the outdoor areas to confirm the cover story to any watching spy satellites.

Once inside, we strolled around the huge hangars bedecked with red Soviet banners urging the workers on to greater efforts on behalf of the motherland. It seemed certain that Bond would abseil down from the roof at any moment in pursuit of a gold-toothed villain. This sensation moved me to remark to the jovial old American from RUSI next to me that: 'I bet your CIA would have loved to have some people inside here in the old days, eh?' To which he responded with a wink and a conspiratorial whisper: 'What makes you think we didn't, young man?'

Being inside Pivdenmash was incredible. They still had some space rockets in production and there was something awe-inspiring about touching them. There was also an eerie feel about a place that had been at the heart of a dark chapter in human history and had now slipped into faded glory. Part of the ghostly atmosphere was physical too – the complex was so vast that it felt deserted even though it was claimed that 13,000 people still worked there.

As the demand for intercontinental ballistic nuclear missiles had dropped off since the end of the Cold War, Pivdenmash had diversified into producing trams and trolleybuses in an attempt to keep the enterprise afloat. That could not help but feel like a fall from grace and the managers who showed us around sounded almost apologetic about it. They tried and failed to look convinced by my suggestion that producing something designed to get people into the city centre, rather than wipe it off the map, was positive progress.

There was little doubt that a workforce that had spent its life building nuclear missiles could easily knock-out a half-decent tram. But the biggest transitional challenge for Pivdenmash was in sales and marketing. This was an institution that had spent its whole history concealing its existence. The managers forlornly acknowledged that they had no clue how to perform a 180 degree turn into advertising their activities and solicited our advice on how to sell their wares. It was not hard to think of a few potential slogans for them but my business studies diploma from Hull College of Further Education had failed woefully to equip me for advising nuclear missile factory managers on how to sell trams.

The Ukrainian President at that time, Leonid Kuchma, had once been the General Director of Pivdenmash. This was surprising because Kuchma, with his stodgy manner and ridiculous comb-over, came across as being no rocket scientist. But behind his dull exterior, he was a cunning and ruthless operator who was willing to plumb the depths to preserve power for himself and his cronies.

The Kuchma regime was notorious for the number of grisly misfortunes suffered by his political and media opponents. One of the worst cases was the murder of Georgiy Gongadze, a courageous investigative journalist who had circumvented the government and oligarch-owned mainstream media by establishing a pioneering online newspaper called *Ukrayinska Pravda*, 'Ukrainian Truth'. The paper had a growing reputation for its reports about high-level corruption and I was trying to arrange a meeting with him to discuss them. But it never happened because on 16th September, 2000 Gongadze was abducted on his way home from work and disappeared. His decapitated and burned corpse was found six weeks later in the woods outside Kiev.

The horrific story took a further twist later that November. I had built up good contacts with Socialist Party leader Alexander Moroz's advisers and one morning they asked me to arrange an urgent meeting with the Ambassador. Moroz turned up soon afterwards with a tape recording, which he was about to make public but had brought to us first. It had apparently been made secretly in Kuchma's office by one of his bodyguards shortly before Gongadze's murder and featured the President luridly cursing the journalist and discussing ways to get rid of him with his Chief of Staff, Volodymyr Litvyn and the Interior Minister, Yuri Kravchenko.

Our Ambassador, among others, was sceptical at first about whether the recording was genuine because he thought that the security on entering the President's office building would have made it too difficult to smuggle in a recording device. As I was able to point out to him when we visited for an unrelated meeting soon afterwards, the security was only tight for visitors – it was barely applied to the insiders who sailed past the metal detectors and scanners in a kerfuffle of jovial greetings with their colleagues on the door.

Time, further evidence and the big circumstantial clue provided by the authorities' ham-fisted attempts to avoid investigating the case properly – at one point Gongadze's body was abducted and disappeared for several weeks - demonstrated that the tape recordings were almost certainly genuine. Something resembling a proper investigation finally got underway after Kuchma left office in early 2005. A few hours before he was due to give evidence that it was rumoured would implicate Kuchma, Kravchenko apparently committed suicide by shooting himself in the head. Twice.

The possibility of an investigation into the Gongadze case arose because of the unexpected victory of the Ukrainian opposition in the 'Orange Revolution'. It brought the pro-democracy candidate, Viktor Yushchenko to power in place of Viktor Yanukovych, the thuggish successor selected by Kuchma, Ukraine's shady business elite and the Russians.

The revolution was a remarkable triumph for the thousands of Ukrainians who camped out in central Kiev for weeks, in sub-zero temperatures, in protest against the initial theft of the election by Yanukovych and his backers. It was also a huge personal achievement for Yushchenko. The previously fit and handsome candidate was poisoned during the campaign with TCDD dioxin, which left him seriously ill and disfigured. His poisoning became apparent after a dinner with a group of senior officials appointed by Kuchma, including, Volodymyr Satsyuk, the Deputy Head of the country's secret security service. Satsyuk now lives in Russia, where he has been granted citizenship and immunity from extradition.

For all that these were deeply unpleasant events, from

a selfish point of view there was great professional interest in working in the Embassy Political Section during the year 2000, when many of the seeds for the subsequent Orange Revolution were sown. Yushchenko was surprisingly appointed Prime Minister by Kuchma, in an attempt by the President to boost his own increasingly scandal-ridden reputation and secure his opponent inside the tent.

Unsurprisingly, a year of friction followed. Yushchenko, at that time, was a notably modest man who did down-to-earth things like driving his own car to work, rather than being ostentatiously chauffeured around in a convoy of black Mercedes like his contemporaries. I accompanied our ambassador to a meeting with him and vividly recall him saying in response to a question about whether he felt at risk: 'Please note, Mr Ambassador, that I am a very careful driver. If I should have an accident, you would be right to be suspicious'. Another prominent Ukrainian opposition leader had recently been killed in a dubious hit and run collision with an unmarked truck that was never traced. Unfortunately for Yushchenko, his diligence could not protect him from poison in his soup.

While the Orange Revolution was unquestionably the triumph of the Ukrainian people bravely fighting to secure their freedom and democratic rights, I like to think that I did everything I could to help those who were already struggling for democracy there, a few years earlier. I was in charge of the Foreign Office's project budget and we made full use of the funds to support numerous civil society organisations. Some were directly relevant to what subsequently happened, such as the organisations that monitored elections and were crucial in providing the evidence that proved the initial 2004 vote had been rigged. The support we provided to other organisations, such as those which campaigned on behalf of disabled children and women forcibly trafficked into the sex trade, helped indirectly by habituating people to waging an organised struggle for their rights. We also had large military and police reform projects which may have played a role in the security forces decision to refrain from firing on the crowds of protesters. In addition, we ran an extensive programme of visits in both directions for journalists and politicians, which enabled the Ukrainians to increase their knowledge of how to function in a democratic environment.

Frankly, all of this ferment was heaven for a global politics nerd like me. One part of my job was to hang around the Verkhovna Rada, the Ukrainian parliament, for which I had a special access pass, chatting to MPs and their staff to find out what was going on. This was my idea of fun, not work. It even carried a hint of a night out in Hull because there was always the chance of a punch-up breaking out, as different factions fought for control of the Speaker's podium. The MPs were a combustible mix of old Communists, new Nationalists, liberal democrats and big time crooks seeking influence and the immunity from prosecution conferred by a seat in parliament. Like any congress, it could be dull when the more obscure issues were being discussed in depth but the Rada certainly had moments when it was the best show in town.

Ukraine's situation as a significant country in the midst of a precarious transition from corrupt authoritarianism to liberal democracy meant that there was a lot of interest in it from British politicians and Members of Parliament. I had more MPs' visits to arrange in Kiev than in any other post in which I have served.

Our Parliamentarians are often criticised for being self-interested and, in the case of overseas trips, always on the look-out for a junket. I wish that I could now produce a string of colourful anecdotes about them behaving badly to confirm that that was the case. But the inconvenient truth is that I found almost all of the numerous MPs, Lords and Ladies that I came across to be well-informed, gracious and professional. It may be because most of my postings were not in places that had obvious junket potential but the majority were admirably committed to playing a useful role in developing UK foreign policy and, in the case of places like Ukraine, to doing what they could to support the development of parliamentary democracy.

That was true even of the Members I was predisposed to dislike for ideological reasons. There was one apparently smug and arrogant Cabinet member who I had loathed dating back to his regular appearances on local television during my formative years in the 1980s who, confusingly for me, muddied his well-earned public reputation for bumptiousness by being a perfect gentleman during a visit as part of the Inter-Parliamentary Union delegation. That was even after I had taken the genteel and rather elderly group of Honourable Members to a bar with fake tiger skin seats, blue neon lighting and a racy clientele. Well they had asked to see somewhere typically Ukrainian.

One member of the delegation was, perhaps, the nicest politician I ever met, the late Lord Biffen. He was getting on in years by then but had earlier in his career, as John Biffen, been a member of Margaret Thatcher's Cabinet. As someone who grew up in the working class north when it was under assault by Thatcher's policies, I fully expected him to have horns. Instead, he was infuriatingly charming and witty. By the last day of the visit, we were chuckling away together on the back seat of the minibus like two kids on a school trip. I am sure there is a useful life lesson in this experience somewhere but, even over a decade later, I am still too traumatised by the experience of liking a senior Tory to work out what it is.

Perhaps the only major management challenge I had with a visiting politician fell into the category of an MP behaving sadly rather than badly. The member in question arrived with the high powered House of Commons Defence Committee. This was an important visit given the contemporary debate about Ukraine potentially joining NATO. I'm sure that there are parliamentary procedural rules that would have made doing otherwise difficult but it seemed to me to be wrong and dangerous that someone who was clearly mired in chronic alcoholism had been allowed to join a delegation to vodka central.

The MP was usually coherent at the start of the day and showed flashes of the wisdom he had once been able to exhibit more regularly. By the afternoon, and in the crafty way of alcoholics, without ever having been seen to consume much booze, he was a disaster area – not unpleasant but slurring and inappropriately verbose. The blackly comic tactic adopted by the other members of the Committee for dealing with this during our official meetings was to sit him next to a large, distinctly Old Labour, Scottish, ex-miner colleague. At any hint of an outburst, he would firmly grab the inebriated one's leg under the table and growl: 'Be quiet, wee man' into his ear. The Scottish MP performed this task with admirable discretion while somehow managing to remain focused on the real matters in hand. But it was still visible to the Ukrainians who, although no strangers to strong drink themselves, looked bemused by the whole business.

My biggest fears throughout the visit were that some catastrophic mishap would befall the alcoholic MP or that he would get lost in the wilds of Kiev. Misplacing an MP on your watch or sending them back to London damaged was detrimental to your career prospects. Each morning I was relieved to find him in the hotel lobby for collection and that he had not gone astray during the night. Somehow I managed to keep him corralled all of the way through the Committee's stay, only to be foiled at the very last moment when he disappeared just as we were about to leave the Embassy for the airport. I quickly roped in a couple of colleagues to help me search frantically for him around the darkening streets of central Kiev. After about half-an-hour I finally found the poor man, who by now looked like a small boy in an old man's body. He was utterly confused, terrified and close to tears.

Betty Boothroyd, the then Madame Speaker of the House of Commons, was an altogether less stressful parliamentary visitor to host. She was a delightful mix of knowledge on how to run a parliament and an old-school showbiz personality. It was a pleasure and a privilege to share the back seat of a Politburo-style Volga limousine with her. Between her visit being arranged and actually taking place, the Speaker's office in the Rada was taken over by the more sinister section linked with crime. It was intriguing to say the least to see Speaker Boothroyd's personal warmth come up against the chill factor of the two deputy speakers of the Rada, who were widely believed to be mafia bosses and carried such an air of evil that, I swear, the temperature dropped by five degrees whenever they walked into a room.

Of all of the political visitors we had, the most impressive was Robin Cook, the Foreign Secretary. A couple of years earlier, I had had an interesting encounter with one of his Special Advisors - who Ministers personally select from outside their Ministry to give them political advice - a few weeks after Cook was appointed. I was showing a friend around the Foreign Office building in London one Sunday and had peeked into the ornate Foreign Secretary's office suite to see if we could have a glance inside. One of the SA's was at work but willingly showed us around. He then, having clearly identified a fellow non-typical FO staffer, sought my advice about dealing with the 'old boys' network' of senior officials. He confided that he and Mr Cook had thought parliament was bad for keeping confidences but they were baffled by the Foreign Office officials' uncanny ability to know everything that Cook and his team had said to each other within minutes of them having done so.

Cook continued to see himself as an outsider in the Foreign Office throughout his time there. He was in the habit, for example, of phoning the relevant desk officer directly whenever he had a question, rather than requesting a formal submission filtered through the Heads of Department and Under Secretaries. Asking the person who dealt with the details of the issue on a daily basis seemed an eminently sensible and efficient way of operating to me, but I know that many members of the senior chain of command did not see it that way.

Cook was renowned for having a sharp mind, which he amply and impressively demonstrated in his meetings with the Ukrainian leadership during his visit to Kiev. He also had a reputation for having a quick temper, something his armed protection officers ruefully confirmed to me during their reconnaissance trip a few weeks before the visit, although they clearly liked him overall.

There was no evidence of this prickliness when he was with us. In fact, the only problem I had with him during the trip made me warm to him even more. As the guardian of the timetable, responsible for making the schedule run to plan, I only had to chase him along once. This was during a short stop we had arranged for him to visit an Embassy project to assist disabled children. I had intended this stop, frankly, to be little more than a brief photo opportunity to publicise the project. Once inside and away from the cameras, Cook totally switched off from politician mode and became engrossed in friendly conversation with the kids and parents. It was a nightmare trying to get him out of there and on to the meeting with President Kuchma for which he was becoming increasingly late. In the end I struggled to do my professional duty because he was clearly enjoying himself and forcing anyone to spend time with Kuchma was cruel.

17. Chernobyl, Babi Yar and Rebrov

WHEN you find out that the opening line of a country's national anthem roughly translates as: 'Ukraine is not dead yet' you sense that its history may not have been an entirely happy one. The Ukrainians' story is perhaps the grimmest in Europe and can seem like an unremitting catalogue of pogrom, famine, genocide, war, occupation and nuclear disaster. Then again, it does mean, that there are no end of fascinating places to visit and people to meet.

Incredibly, one reactor at the Chernobyl nuclear power plant was still running and supplying electricity until the year I was there, in 2000, despite the massive disaster that had befallen the plant fourteen winters earlier. Apart from the rickety reactor that was still in use, the plant was a great source of concern because the one that had exploded had been hastily covered with a concrete sarcophagus that was crumbling and starting to leak. I can't say that it was a daily worry for me but there was the occasional nervous twinge when you noticed the iodine tablets in your bathroom cabinet. We were supposed to take them to protect ourselves from thyroid cancer if there was ever another major leak. Some odd sounding advice also used to come around periodically, such as swimming from the beaches on the islands in the middle of the Dniepr River that runs through Kiev only being advisable if you made sure not to touch the bottom. This was because the radiation had attached itself to the heavy metals that also polluted the river and had sunk to its bed with them.

One of our tasks in the Embassy was to monitor the use of the international funds allocated for building a new, more secure structure to entomb the radioactive material at Chernobyl. We also obtained some equipment for the scientific laboratory that monitored radioactivity and studied its effects on the surrounding region. The lab is located inside the thirty kilometre exclusion zone around the plant, where no-one is allowed to live because the radiation levels are so high that human life will not be safe there for the next 20,000 years. Someone needed to deliver our gift there and, surprisingly, I was the only volunteer for the job.

Visiting the Chernobyl exclusion zone, with its ghost towns that have been left exactly as they were on the day of evacuation, was a fascinating experience. The scientists at the laboratory were clearly stimulated by having the then unique opportunity to study the world's only existing empirical example of the effects of radiation on life and the environment. They were particularly absorbed by the way in which nature had surprisingly reasserted itself in the zone, with deer and other wildlife flourishing in the absence of people despite the toxic environment.

The most astounding stories were about the acts of heroism that took place during the disaster. I was awestruck when visiting the modest Chernobyl Museum in Kiev to learn how the firemen and workers who fought the fire and secured the highly radioactive material before it harmed even more people had done so without adequate protective clothing and in the knowledge that they were condemning themselves to an agonising early death.

The museum was located in Podil, a lively and attractive district in the lower town down the hill from the city centre. It was home to many Jewish inhabitants until the Second World War. That ended after the Germans captured Kiev on 19 September, 1941. Just over a week later the Jews were marched from the suburb, and other parts of the city, to the Babi Yar ravine a couple of miles away. There they were forced to surrender their valuables and take off their clothes. They were then pushed towards the edge of the ditch in groups of ten and shot by Nazi soldiers, aided by German and Ukrainian policemen. After two days of shooting, the bodies of 33,771 Jews filled the ravine and were covered with a thin layer of dirt. This was the biggest single massacre of the Holocaust and was followed over the next few months by the killing of thousands more Jews, Gypsies, and Soviet prisoners of war. In all, over 100,000 people were murdered at Babi Yar.

Babi Yar is now part of a quiet, wooded park in Kiev. The ravine looks exactly as it did in the photographs from September 1941, minus the bodies. But if you have seen those photos and heard the story, the bodies are sickeningly vivid in your mind when you stand there.

Thankfully not everywhere in Ukraine is as desperately grim as Chernobyl and Babi Yar, even if the dark history of Europe's hinterlands between West and East lies under the surface everywhere if you look. Kiev itself is an attractive, vibrant city with its centre perched on a hill overlooking the river. It has grand boulevards, spectacular ancient churches and numerous good bars, clubs and restaurants, many of which spill out into the streets during the warm summer.

Lviv, in the west of the country, is similarly appealing and Odessa in the south has a unique place in Russian and Ukrainian cultural history. The city's glory days as an important European port and trading centre with a melting pot population are long gone but it retains a dilapidated charm and a deserved reputation for wit and wide-boys. After a few days in Odessa, you start to find it normal to see someone walking an albino crocodile on a lead down the main street.

Somewhat off the tourist trail, such as it is, I also used to like visiting Donetsk, the main city in the Donbass coal and steel region that once formed the heart of the Soviet Union's industrial might. I have always had a curious affection for broken down industrial hell-holes which may owe something to my upbringing. I gather that Donetsk has been spruced up since I was last there but at the time it was the finest example I had yet seen. It had slagheaps in the city centre, grime everywhere and, despite, sitting on top of all that fuel, patchy electricity and very few working street lights at night.

Part of my affection for the place may have stemmed from my first visit there. It involved travelling a short distance out of town to check on an environmental project the Embassy had initiated before my arrival to preserve the Steppe moorland. I arrived on the overnight train from Kiev at the crack of dawn on a brisk minus 20 degree February morning. My lack of knowledge about nature meant that my check to see that the wild horses and grass were all present and correct was equally brisk.

The farmer running the project and I then retired to his cosy farmhouse for breakfast. After porridge and toast, he produced a bottle of his finest home-produced vodka. Many Ukrainians find regular vodka to be a vapid, unsatisfying brew and like to pep it up by distilling it with chili peppers.

It was the first time I had tasted it and I can certainly vouch for its warming properties on winter's morning. Once my eyeballs returned to their sockets and the steam stopped coming out of my ears, I also learned that there are few more satisfying ways to spend a working day than swopping stories with a Ukrainian farming family while getting steadily plastered in front of their roaring log fire. Travel does indeed broaden the mind, even when scrambling it.

My affinity for Donetsk was further enhanced by the discovery that several of the young Ukrainians who worked in our British Council office there had learnt English on a twin-town exchange programme at Barnsley College. This meant that they spoke excellent English in a perfect South Yorkshire accent. Some of them even had the blunt character typical of the town and it engendered in me a pleasingly off-kilter feeling of being so close, yet so far from home.

Another native of the Donbass region that I enjoyed meeting in Ukraine was Serhiy Rebrov, the Dynamo Kiev striker who was at the time the leading scorer in Champions League history and one of the hottest properties in world football. He had somewhat surprisingly just agreed to join the then mid-table Tottenham Hotspur, rather than one of the big European powers such as AC Milan, where his former striking partner Andriy Shevchenko was now playing. I was nearly as taken aback when he and his wife agreed to my request to be interviewed over dinner for the Embassy magazine.

The reasons for his choice of club soon became apparent when we spoke. Rather than being the confident superstar footballer I had been expecting, Rebrov was a quiet, shy and sheltered young man. He had been cloistered in the tightly controlled Dynamo Kiev set up since his mid-teens, where everything was structured and arranged for the players, who often lived in shared club housing at their training camp until well into adulthood. Before then, he had grown up as the son of a miner in a small Donbass pit town - a region that makes Donetsk look like Las Vegas and where it is not uncommon for over a hundred poorly paid miners a year to die in industrial accidents.

He freely admitted that he had signed for Tottenham because, once Dynamo had told him they were ready to cash-in and sell him, Spurs had been the first to put a contract and signing-on fee on the table. He also attributed his anaemic form during the last few months of the Ukrainian season to his being terrified of getting injured and blowing the chance of earning more money than he and his family had ever imagined possible. It was then no great surprise that one of the greatest talents in world football subsequently sank with barely a trace in the big city and brash atmosphere of a British dressing room.

My dinner invitation to Rebrov was a small example of how I had learned that being a diplomat conferred some status upon me and Ukraine was the place where I perfected the art of turning a Diplomatic ID card into an access all areas pass. I realised that in many parts of the world an irrelevant but official pass, a confident stride and an air of polite impatience can get you in almost anywhere. My flat in Kiev was next to the National Opera House and a short walk from the Olympisky national stadium.

On a boring Tuesday night before big European football games, I would often go to the stadium, flash my pass confidently at the security guards and sit in on the press conference of the visiting club manager before going down to pitch-side to watch the team train. Much to the pleasure of my Auntie Sue, a Manchester United fan, we did this when both she and they were in town and got some nice pictures of her and my mum hugging Sir Alex Ferguson on the massive pitch.

Kiev was also the place where I had my only experience of handling guns, which is not one I have rushed to repeat. The first activity of a colleague's stag weekend was to go clay pigeon shooting at a club on the edge of the city. I was outstandingly hopeless at it but the shotguns had a salutary feeling of power and violence about them because the recoil nearly knocked your shoulder off when you fired them. That was not the case with the surprise 'treat' that followed. We were taken around the back to a large barn and given AK-47 machine guns to fire at piles of tin cans. It was a terrifying experience. The guns fire off a ridiculous number of rounds at impossible speed and in goodness knows what direction, while feeling as light and insubstantial as a child's toy. Rather than fun, I left with a disturbing sense of how easy it was for such lethal weapons to be used to kill and maim without any feeling or sensation at all.

All in all, Ukraine was quite a year-long experience, and somehow I managed to dodge a return to London again by picking up another short notice posting in Brussels, which would prove calmer and even more satisfying.

18. Jeux Sans Frontieres

A STANDARD piece of Foreign Office wisdom I heard repeatedly when posted to the UK Permanent Representation (UKRep) to the European Union in 2001 was that three years in Brussels was enough to turn the most ardent Europhile into a raving Eurosceptic. Rather like a sausage-lover being forced to watch their manufacture, the theory was that close exposure to the inefficiencies of the EU Institutions and the tedious bickering in endless meetings with other member states would alienate even the most consummate diplomat.

Perhaps because I was not a consummate diplomat, that turned out to be wrong in my case. Despite being thoroughly exposed to the grisly workings of the Brussels frankfurter factory, I left a convinced European.

This unexpected outcome was partly because, on a professional level, I appreciated the chance to learn about how the EU worked from the inside. Indeed, I wished that it had come earlier because understanding better would have been useful in every previous job I had done in the Diplomatic Service. More importantly, my time in Brussels gave me a much greater appreciation of the value of the Union and its historic impact.

None of these positive impressions, though, stemmed directly from my day-to-day experience of working in Brussels. As my wife would confirm, I moaned endlessly about my job there. Like all member state officials posted to our EU representations, I spent inordinate amounts of time sitting in meetings listening to fifteen, and, in the last year of my posting, after new members states joined, twenty-five, national delegates explaining their detailed positions on some obscure EU project or regulation, which then had to somehow be brought together into a consensus that everyone could accept.

I had a number of standard tactics for getting through these meetings such as reading magazines concealed in my briefing papers or treating them as a live French lesson by switching to the simultaneous interpretation on my headphones. Never before, too, has the prospect of a lunch-time bag of chips been fantasised over at such length. But, then, the chips are pretty good in Belgium.

My specific role was as a Commercial Officer. The purpose of the Commercial Section in a typical Embassy is to help UK firms to take advantage of the business opportunities in the country concerned and to stimulate inward investment into the UK by that country's companies. In the untypical case of UKRep, which is, in effect, an Embassy to an organisation rather than a country, I was tasked with helping British businesses to profit from the commercial opportunities generated by EU budgets and spending programmes.

By far the greatest number of opportunities arose from the EU's external aid programmes, which provide hundreds of millions of Euros to help non-EU countries improve their governance and economic development. Most of the aid is provided in the form of projects run by European consultants earning commercial rates on contracts awarded by competitive tender. While many of them were undoubtedly worthwhile, I always found it hard to argue with the complaints of many in the beneficiary countries that the external aid programmes mostly recycled EU money back into the hands of European consultants, rather than really investing it in the countries concerned.

As a believer in the value of well-targeted and administered aid, I struggled with a feeling of distaste at being asked to find ways to help businessmen profit from these programmes. This feeling was probably not helped by some of the ways in which we did so. One method was to use our privileged official position to obtain 'in-confidence' project documents while they were at the preparation stage and use them to give UK businesses early warning of contract tenders that would be coming up. The fact that our colleagues from other EU member states were all up to the same vaguely disreputable thing was not enough to make it feel like an edifying way to spend my days.

My discomfort reached its pinnacle during the Iraq War, when I was despatched to attend EU meetings on a potential aid programme for the country. Like many people, I'd had misgivings about the war and was appalled by how it turned out. Even so, I think I could have squared this had I been going to the meetings to help develop the best possible reconstruction programme for Iraq. Instead, I was there to sniff out opportunities for British companies in the country that we had played our part in pulverising, a task for which I had no enthusiasm whatsoever and which provided one of the few instances during my Diplomatic Service career when I wondered whether I was really in the right line of work.

Conversely, trawling for money-grubbing opportunities in the wreckage of Iraq on behalf of UK companies inadvertently produced one of the minor accomplishments of which I am most proud in my career. My role in Brussels meant that my name appeared as a contact point for advice on the government's UK Trade & Investment website. One day I received a message from an Iraqi engineer who had alighted on them, requesting help in his desperate struggle to find work in order to feed his family during the violent chaos of the occupation and civil war in his homeland. Helping with such enquiries was not remotely part of my job description. But in the spirit of human decency at a time when we were being deluged with distressing images from there and, no doubt, also to salve my troubled conscience, I spent some time putting together a list of appropriate contacts at British companies operating in Iraq and sent it to him. Several months later I cried when I received a further e-mail from him offering profuse thanks because he had followed up with the recommendations and had obtained not one, but two, good jobs.

In diplomacy, it is usually difficult to discern with any certainty what positive effect your work as a small cog in the big wheel of foreign policy has had on situations that are often open-ended and inconclusive by their nature. Even though I have worked on much higher profile, bigger issues, it was a wonderful feeling to know that I had been able to do something unequivocally useful for someone in a difficult situation. Somewhat tangentially, this distant contact with warfare and the havoc it wreaks on decent, hardworking people enhanced my appreciation of how the development of the EU had transformed an entire continent from battle-torn destitution to peace and prosperity.

This view began to form during one of the first tourist trips I made after being posted to Brussels, when I visited the First World War cemeteries and museums around the Belgian town of Ypres. There, the names of thousands of young people from backgrounds just like mine are recorded on immaculate, sombre memorials and gravestones. As I walked around absorbing their senseless deaths, I was overwhelmed by the feeling that there can be few sadder places on earth.

In many ways, the First World War was merely a continuation of the way relations had been conducted in Europe for centuries. Shifting alliances between countries were regularly punctuated by brutal wars prompted by squabbles about territory and resources. The difference when the First World War broke out was that military technology had advanced sufficiently to kill millions rather than thousands. The post-war horror at what had happened gave rise to the famous slogan 'Never Again'. Unfortunately, nothing practical was put in place to break the cycle of conflict. It turned out to be 'yet again' twenty years later, when ongoing rivalry, economic crisis and the rise of fascism led to World War II and over sixty million more deaths.

After that, radical changes were finally made in Europe, inspired by statesmen such as Winston Churchill, Konrad Adenauer, Robert Schuman and Jean Monnet. The most significant was the establishment of the forerunner to the EU, the European Coal and Steel Community. The founding fathers of the EU saw the pooling of resources in the mutual interest and structured, rules-based cooperation as the way to avoid more conflict. The outcome of their vision has been a staggering success. Six decades on, there have been no further wars between EU members. In fact, the very notion of such a thing seems ridiculous in 2014, even at a time of economic crisis.

Every nation that has joined the Union, which has grown into the biggest, most successful single market the world has ever seen, has increased its long-term prosperity as a result. The attraction of membership has helped democracy and freedom to spread across the continent, from the destroyed and defeated World War II fascist dictatorships of Italy and Germany, to countries like Spain and Portugal, where such regimes endured longer, and the nations of Central Europe that spent decades in the grip of Soviet communism.

To someone like me who had grown up during the Cold War and started his overseas career in Eastern Europe soon after the collapse of communism, it seemed incredible that the countries of the once dark and mysterious East were being reunited with the rest of Europe so quickly. It was a privilege to be in Brussels to witness this historic realignment when eight former Eastern Bloc nations joined the Union in 2004. Even ravaged Romania was well on the way to membership by then (it joined in 2007) – something I would not have bet a single Euro cent on happening when I had lived there a decade earlier.

The bulk of the immense credit due for turning countries such as Poland, the Czech Republic and Estonia from post-communist basket cases into thriving liberal democracies in such a short space of time belongs to their people and politicians. But the invitation held out to join the EU also played a huge role in these countries successful transition. Almost all previous attempts to bring Europe together have been made by force, involving great drama and bloodshed and always ending in disaster. The EU achieved infinitely better results via a painstaking bureaucratic process of aligning laws, regulations and governance systems. Dull it might be, but if ever a continent needed to cut down on drama it was Europe and the Union has proved to be a stunningly effective mechanism.

Some English nationalists and their continental

counterparts tie themselves in knots trying to claim that the EU has had little to do with these great advances. But the truth is that an organisation expressly designed to end war, spread freedom and increase prosperity in Europe has, against all historical precedent, fulfilled all of those objectives.

The history that led to the formation of the EU and the fate of previous generations who were sent to mainland Europe to pursue Britain's interests, was often in the back of my mind when I was stuck in meetings in Brussels. True to form, we argued endlessly with our fellow Europeans and never got everything we wanted. But rather than suffering the hell of war, our encounters took place in bland meeting rooms. It might have been hellishly boring but it wasn't the sodden trenches. And, in the end, we always got a deal our countries could live with. Best of all, nobody died and none of our names were ever going to be inscribed on a monument to fallen heroes.

19. An Ideal Home

ASIDE from learning to love the EU, there turned out to be many other reasons to enjoy living in Brussels. But these reasons were not immediately apparent when my wife-to-be and I arrived there. To the distress of her feet, I insisted, as always, that the best way to get to know a new place was to take a long walk through it. What we found during our early strolls was a city that was in need of a good scrub, filled with broken cobblestones and epic quantities of dog muck.

Such unpromising initial impressions are not uncommon among new arrivals in the Belgian capital. They are frequently compounded by dismal weather and that the first sights many see are either the run-down streets around the Gare du Midi Eurostar terminal, the ugly business district or the monolithic EU quarter.

Brussels' unkempt appearance extends all the way up to the Royal Palace, with its grimy walls and net curtains that would have had my grandmothers' tutting about them being overdue a wash. But, over time, the general air of shabbiness came to embody the relaxed, lived-in atmosphere that made me feel more at home in Brussels than any other place I have resided outside of Hull. The other slow-burn reason was that further exploration revealed the city to be down-to-earth yet quirkily distinctive with a rich variety of people, places and possibilities.

That part is, perhaps, best illustrated by an early encounter I had with a transvestite in the Gare du Midi toilets. I had not bumped into many before and previously imagined them to be tall, lean, thoroughly glammed-up Ru Paul types from the Rio carnival or clubs of Manhattan. Not in Brussels. This one was working as a caretaker in the gents. He was short, chubby and dressed in a grubby cleaner's outfit, with heavy, smudged make-up, three-day stubble and a roll-up cigarette hanging from the corner of his mouth. Les Dawson's gossipy old lady Ada was Brigitte Bardot by comparison. Absurd, earthy and utterly individual – Madame Mop was Brussels to a tee.

Such encounters confirmed that, having long missed the offbeat atmosphere of Bucharest, I had made the right choice in coming to the home of the surrealist art movement. As a Northerner, I also quickly identified with Belgium's lack of ostentation and self-deprecating sense of humour. Despite the international profile conferred on it by the presence of the EU and NATO, Brussels is refreshingly short on great world city pretensions and gigantic glass shards making bombastic architectural statements. Indeed, the Belgians generally are not big on blowing their own saxophone, despite the instrument having been invented there by Adolphe Sax.

The absence of stridency was on show during the first Belgian national day celebrations the good lady and I attended in Brussels. Rather than being an orgy of patriotism and showcase of national potency, it featured probably the least intimidating military parade I have ever witnessed. We gathered eagerly by the side of the road to see the full might of the Belgian armed forces. What transpired was a very brief procession by several ageing armoured cars and a gaggle of droopily moustachioed gents in uniform apparently ambling from the bar to the chip stand. It looked like an outing by the paramilitary wing of the traffic wardens. May Day on Red Square it was not.

The clichéd 'name ten famous Belgians' jibe is another by-product of the country's diffidence. There are in fact quite a few of them for a country of its size. But it is often assumed by outsiders that they are either French or Dutch, a misapprehension that extends even to resoundingly Belgian specialities like French fries. A good explanation of this phenomenon appears in Harry Pearson's entertaining tribute to Belgium, *A Tall Man in a Low Land* when an exasperated local tells him that the difference between his countrymen and their brash Dutch neighbours: 'Can be seen in cheese. Here we make many different kinds of great cheeses but nobody outside of Belgium has heard of them. The Dutch make one kind of very tasteless cheese and they make sure all the world knows about it'.

Foreigners can be forgiven for not having a particularly high opinion of Belgium because neither do many of the natives. If recent election results are anything to go by, almost half of them would like to abolish their own country. Many are supporters of the separatist, nationalist movement in Flanders, the Dutch-speaking Northern half of the country. In the region around Brussels, which, nowadays, is a mostly French-speaking city, the language boundary bisects the suburbs. Most of the disputes seem to be trivial spats about people from one side of the street being denied the right to speak French in the Post Office on the Dutch-speaking side of the road.

The issue underlying the discord is that some Flemish people feel that their culture and language were long suppressed by the French speaking Walloons from the Southern half of the country. Now that they have been left as top dogs by the decline of the heavy industry that fuelled Wallonia's dominance, many Flemings resent, as they see it, being asked to support their Francophone countrymen financially.

Even allowing for the deeper subtexts, the language squabbles that are the everyday manifestation of them still seemed bizarrely petty to an outsider like me. Having grown-up as a typically monoglot Brit, I have always been inordinately impressed by multilingualism and found it sad that a country, so language-rich that one tiny area of Brussels – Marolles - has its own dialect, was retreating from it.

Still, if the upshot of Belgium's fractious politics was a well-developed sense of modesty and underwhelming displays of pomp and ceremony, then that was fine by me. I am discomfited by jingoism and found Belgium's strong streak of individuality a much more attractive characteristic. It is no accident that many of their famous sons and daughters are, in fact, creative trailblazers such as the legendary torch singer, Jacques Brel; the great detective fiction writer, Georges Simenon; surrealist artist, René Magritte; Art Nouveaux designer, Victor Horta; filmmakers, the Dardenne brothers, and fashion designers such as Martin Margiela and Dries van Noten, among many others.

Nor is this creative spirit confined to the rarefied world of the arts. The Flemish, in particular, are said to be born with 'a brick in their stomachs' and are deeply attached to building their own houses. Inevitably, some of them are better at it than others but, for someone from a place consisting largely of uniform estates, there is beauty in coming across towns and villages where no two dwellings are the same. I could never be described as a DIY fanatic but even I was impressed to discover that Belgian DIY stores stock a full range of bricks, breezeblocks and roof tiles along with the usual screws, taps and chipboard shelves.

When filling in the time between house-building projects, many Belgians are incorrigible tinkerers. This leads to some strange bicycle contraptions causing bother on the roads and a bewildering array of beers made from concoctions that make no sense in theory but work resoundingly well in practice.

I was fortunate enough to get closely acquainted with the ale because my wife got a job with the world's biggest brewer. For a lad from my background, having a girlfriend that works for the brewery is the definition of living the dream – although her appointment had no bearing on our decision to get married soon afterwards. The terms of her employment included a monthly ale allowance direct from the warehouse. Aside from being the mother of all perks, that took care of my father's Christmas present during the three years we were there. I never ceased to be giddily impressed on my visits to her office by the tea-point fridges being filled with a large variety of bottled beers, rather than just a carton of milk and a mouldy sandwich. They even had free, self-service draught taps in convenient locations around the building. It seemed an off-beat approach to staff welfare and one could only imagine the carnage if any employer tried something similar back home.

Idiosyncrasy is built-in to the geography of Brussels, which is made up of nineteen distinctly different Communes. Somehow it has time-warped itself into an era before the corporate takeover of globalisation. Although there are chain stores in the main shopping districts, elsewhere almost all of the shops, cafes, bars and restaurants are individually owned and have their own character as a result. Amid the array of butchers, bakers and chocolate makers, the throwback feel is enhanced by things like the tiny, family-run car dealerships with stocks of three vehicles in converted downstairs floors of terraced town houses and miniature petrol stations on residential street corners that have been there since Stirling Moss was still playing with his Scalextric.

Brussels' array of unique eating and drinking establishments, in particular, provide a great antidote to the globalised sameness that is increasingly a feature of travel in the modern world. As a consequence, with the possible exception of the main tourist trap areas, your odds of getting a good meal, across the full-range of the price spectrum, are better than almost anywhere else in the world. We found more great places to eat in the square kilometre around our flat in the Commune of Ixelles that there had been in the whole of London when I lived there in the late 'eighties and early 'nineties. Some of the best were simple neighbourhood places, such as Le Chatelain du Liban, a Lebanese restaurant on the corner of Place du Chatelain and its near neighbour, the equally imaginatively named Le Chatelain pub. They served a phenomenal Pavé of steak - named after the French word for cobblestone, which it matched in shape and size - chips and choice of sauces, grilled on an open fire at the back of the bar. The only drawback was that, in typically relaxed Brussels fashion, it only seemed to be open for about three hours on the second Tuesday of every month, so you had to be alert and get in there whenever the shutters went up. The only occasion when it was guaranteed to be open was market day on the square outside, which was a gourmet feast in itself. On summer market day afternoons, the tiny place seemed to be serving top notch beer to thousands of people as they spilled out of its doors and formed a disorderly queue by the rotisserie chicken stall.

An even more laid-back establishment was the small African restaurant owned and run by Tony Coulibaly, a recently retired Senegalese itinerant professional footballer, who had used his savings from his career at various Belgian clubs and other outposts, such as Linfield in Northern Ireland, to open up his own place. He was charm personified and a smashing cook but his grasp of kitchen logistics left something to be desired. It was open plan to allow the customers to see the chef in action and Tony to continue chatting to them from behind the counter. It was an entertaining theatre of chaos.

The first time my wife and I went there with some friends, we were baffled by the look of terror that took over Tony's naturally smiling face whenever we ordered something from the menu. It was followed by much banging of kitchen cupboard doors and a frantic shout-whispered conversation with his sous-chef, who would then exit at speed through the back door. Initially, we thought that the underling had stormed out following a row and feared for our dinner. But we were reassured when he returned ten minutes later panting, perspiring and clutching a couple of carrier bags. When the exercise was repeated after almost every order, we realised that Tony and his sidekick's cooking skills were not matched by their stock keeping and that they were constantly running off for supplies. It all tasted as fresh as you would expect though.

Fabulous though the food and drink is, there is much more to Brussels. Its general appearance may not be postcard perfect and it does have a surprising amount, for a major European city, of derelict buildings. But there are numerous places of astonishing beauty, even in close proximity to the run down grot. The most obvious example in the centre of town is the breathtaking Grand Place and atmospheric narrow, restaurant-lined streets around the Petit Rue du Bouchers, which are great to stroll through even if you are best advised to eat elsewhere. This is tourist central yet still features some great finds such as the cinema and bookshops in the old Arenberg Galeries. The terrific bars around Place St. Géry and antique shops of Sablon are a short walk away, as are the excellent museums and galleries of the Mont des Arts. Away from the centre, Brussels offers delights such as the distinctively elegant Art Nouveaux town houses around where we lived in Ixelles and St Gilles, the grand mansions of Parc Woluwe and the beautiful wooded parkland in the Bois de la Cambre.

It has an excellent music scene, being a large enough city with a range of good venues to make it a fixture on most tour itineraries but small enough to ensure all concerts are easily accessible. My favourite annual event was the Couleur Café festival, which brings together some great musicians from all over the world for three days every summer. It is typically Bruxellois in that it is held in a dilapidated former warehouse and goods yard complex, manageable in scale and mellow in atmosphere. The layout makes it easy to wander between the three different stages via a mouthwatering variety of food stands and eccentric arts and entertainment displays.

The world-fest of Couleur Café is a by-product of Brussels' greatest treasure - the way it has quietly welcomed people from all corners of the planet with its uncanny knack of making them feel at home. This allowed us to meet some wonderful, fascinating characters; from Rwandans who had escaped the recent genocide in their country, to Cubans in their tiny bar near the Grand Place, complete with its authentically aged and virtuoso, Buena Vista-style musicians shoehorned in the corner, and the extrovert steakhouse proprietor who had been forced to flee for her life from Chile, where she was a Socialist Mayor until General Pinochet's murderous 1973 coup.

In return, such people gave Brussels the numerous, intimately proportioned neighbourhoods with distinct ethnic flavours that are a rich part of its fabric. On my short journey to work alone, I would walk past the Portuguese cafes on the way down to Place Flagey, were the former public radio company building had been converted into an impressive cultural centre, and on through a friendly Moroccan district.

On the way back, I would come through Matongé, which was named after a central area of Kinshasa, the capital of the Democratic Republic of Congo, from where many of its residents hail. By day Matongé is filled with women shopping for plantains and cassava, conducting voluble conversations while getting extravagant braided hair-do's in the salons and generally treating the streets as an extension of their living rooms. Later on, a summer evening in Matongé is a joy to behold. Even by African standards, the Congolese are loud and lively – and that is just the men's clothes. If you have been keeping a scarlet tartan suit, leopard print Stetson and ostrich leather shoes in your wardrobe for just the right occasion, then Matongé is the place to head for. The Congolese Sapeur culture involves the men trying to outdo each other for garish yet stylish attire and makes for an unparalleled people-watching spectacle as they promenade around a neighbourhood throbbing with infectious Congolese music.

The dark side of Belgian history is the tie that binds Matongé to the mansions of Woluwe and many grand, old public buildings and institutions throughout Belgium. Many of the latter were built with fortunes extracted during Belgium's colonial possession of Congo, Rwanda and

Burundi, which was perhaps the most disgraceful episode in the inglorious history of European colonisation of Africa.

From 1885 to 1908, Congo was, uniquely in colonial history, the personal property of Belgium's King Leopold II. The colony was secured for him by the famous explorer Henry Morton Stanley of: 'Dr. Livingstone, I presume?' fame. Leopold created the façade of a high-minded environmental research project to cover up his true purpose, which was to extract the much sought after rubber, ivory and other natural resources of Congo for his own benefit. By some estimates, substantiated by documents from the time, up to ten million Congolese were either murdered or worked to death by Leopold's private army in pursuit of the colony's riches. His agents also committed countless rapes, used limb amputation to punish workers who failed to meet their unattainable demands and were responsible for mass kidnapping, looting and village burning. Adam Hochschild's book *King Leopold's Ghost* provides perhaps the best account of the whole terrible period.

Details of the horror eventually began to leak out and were considered shameful enough even by the low standards of the early twentieth century for the Belgian government to buy the colony from their King in 1908. However, returning it to the people it actually belonged to clearly did not occur to anyone at the time. Congo was then run by the Belgian state in a marginally less brutal fashion until the former Brussels-Matongé resident, Patrice Lumumba, led a successful struggle for independence in 1960. He was murdered soon afterwards by a shady network of Belgians, Congolese rivals and other enemies.

When we were in Brussels in the early 2000s, the state-funded Royal Museum for Central Africa, located in beautiful grounds in the suburb of Tervuren, was still maintaining the fiction that the whole horrific Belgian colonial misadventure had been a well-meaning ecological project and paid tribute to the heroic Belgians who had selflessly brought civilisation to their part of Africa. There was no mention of the seventy-five years of looting, the murder of millions of Africans or even how this supposed civilising enterprise came to leave the vast nation with less than 30 university graduates by the time of independence. Interestingly for me, our stay in Brussels coincided with a proper debate finally breaking out in Belgium about the truth of its colonial past and this horribly dark chapter in the country's history was at long last being acknowledged.

The modern, post-colonial Belgian state is a rather more attractive entity. Despite the country's dishevelled appearance and the presence of several more layers of government than is necessary for optimum efficiency, most essential public services work well. Not least among these is the health service, as we discovered when our first child was born in Brussels, thus securing for us a lifelong connection to the city. The hospital, Edith Cavell - named after a heroic British nurse who worked in Belgium during World War I and treated patients from all sides before being executed by the Germans for helping two hundred Allied soldiers to escape - was excellent. It was unflashy but well-equipped, with plentiful and highly capable staff.

The tone of no-nonsense competence was set by the forceful obstetrician-gynaecologist who looked after my wife throughout her pregnancy. She made no bones about being there solely to look after the mother and child. As the birth date approached, she made clear to me that, while she was reluctantly prepared to tolerate fathers in the delivery room, she would not stand for any distracting squeamishness. She had astutely identified a faint-hearted father-to-be because even I was unconvinced by my sworn promises to be stoic. Thankfully I just about managed to keep up appearances and our son has been a wonderful souvenir of the city ever since.

Before we managed to establish our own connection by birth right, I used football, as always, to integrate myself into Belgian life. Rather than joining one of the proliferation of British clubs, I signed up with FC Ramblers, an entirely Belgian outfit that was looking for players. This was a great way of getting acquainted with like-minded people and escaping the expatriate bubble that exists in Brussels. It was also a good way to improve my rudimentary French, starting, inevitably, with swear words which were mostly limited to speculation about the virtue of your protagonist's mother.

Belgium is not generally considered to be Latin but it is often referred to, mostly by its indigenous population as, Europe's most northerly Latin country. Evidence came in the dressing room before my first game. I was one of the first to arrive and sat quietly at the far end to weigh up my new colleagues as they came in. The first, somewhat alarming, observation I made was that it was standard practice for each player to greet his teammates with a kiss on each cheek. That had not been a big part of my footballing education in the Hull Sunday League, where any greeting more uninhibited then a growl was considered irredeemably camp.

On to the pitch, I was stereotyped horribly. It was assumed that, being English, I would be good at tackling, heading and hoofing the ball unfeasible distances, so they stuck me at centre-half. In reality, I had none of these attributes but was too keen for a game and too inarticulate in French to argue.

In the end, everything worked out rather well and I enjoyed my football in Brussels as much as anywhere I have ever played. As a team, we were nothing special but they were a great bunch of lads to be around. And, it turned out that, in my central defensive partner, Patrick Van Driessen, they already had the classic English centre-half they were looking for. Patrick was a delight to play alongside in that he enthusiastically threw himself at everything with a swashbuckling disregard for personal safety. His first two touches in any given situation were invariably a miscued flying header followed by a two-footed tackle. This left me, in a complete role reversal from what the captain had envisaged, to mimic an old-school continental libero by picking up loose balls from among the dismembered limbs before classily distributing them to our midfielders. In keeping with the retro feel, we also operated a man-for-man marking system, the one-on-one combat element of which I surprised myself by finding as much fun as doing anything creative, especially on the two separate occasions when my opponent, an Italian and a Portuguese, upped and skulked off the pitch in frustration. I have to admit, though, that the infamous gluey Belgian mud and incessant rain was a big help in this task. It slowed everybody down to my pace and kept even the speediest young whippersnappers within discreet ankle-tapping range.

Watching football was fun too and taught me that the Belgian flair for food stretches to some unlikely places. Only in Belgium would it feel normal to find a kiosk selling freshly cooked snails in garlic butter next to the burger van, as was the case behind the popular side of RSC Anderlecht's Parc Astrid football ground.

To be fair, Anderlecht are the aristocrats of Belgian football and earthier experiences are easy to find. The closest club to home was Union Saint-Gilloise, who had dominated the game before World War II but had long since been confined to the third division. Their stadium is a study in past glory. Once inside, it was easy to envisage the packed pre-war crowds from the old photos because the only structural change over the last seventy years is the steady reclamation of the upper terracing by the forest that surrounds the ground.

The club I quickly adopted, though, was Standard Liege, from a tough town that would be entirely at home in the North of England. Their ground, Sclessin, is a cauldron surrounded by steelworks and a great place to watch football. In typical working-class style, the fans are a passionate bunch, proud of their loudly expressed left-wing and anti-racist politics. Soon after arriving in Belgium, I was charmed by an interview with one of Standard's leading ultras, who sought to divert attention from some recent misbehaviour by boasting about the unusual diversity of his hooligan gang, saying: 'We've got Italians, Africans, four Arabs and even a Jew'. You sometimes have to wonder whether we have got the wrong people running the Middle East Peace Process.

For Standard fans, their overriding demand in return for their hard-earned ticket money and vociferous backing is that the players get some sweat on the shirt. And they are not shy about taking action if they feel short-changed. I was amused to witness the fans, after one lacklustre away performance, blockading the team coach in the stadium car park. The trapped players were politely informed by the supporters that they had wasted two hours of the fans' time, so they would now be returning the favour.

For all of its endearing eccentricities, down-to-earth familiarity and homely shabbiness, Brussels captured me most of all because it still managed to embody the glamorous, continental abroad I had imagined as a youngster. At the end of our street, where the French shop signs of the cobbled Rue Bailli met the elegant buildings of Avenue Louise, the trams clattering by and yellow tinged street lighting made me expect to see Jean-Paul Belmondo hurry by in a perfectly tailored raincoat on his way to a romantic assignation. Better still, once I had invested in a raincoat and had my own stylish, spirited woman in our apartment, it was easily possible to imagine that I was him.

For a lad from Hull, it felt like I had stepped through Redifusion's window on Prospect Street and into an impossibly exotic French film from the 'sixties.

20. Moscow Calling

MY wife and I were both Russian speakers with a long-standing fascination for the country. Consequently, we jumped at the chance of a posting there when our time in Brussels came to an end.

In a characteristic example of her drive, individuality and intelligence, her Russophilia stemmed from her decision to learn the language as a fun aside to her main studies at University. Equally typically, my interest originated in a drunken weekend with my mates.

Whilst I was working in Dubai, several of my closest Foreign Office friends were posted in Russia or elsewhere in the former Soviet Union. That made Moscow the ideal location for an Easter weekend get together, which was joined by my brother and another mate from Hull.

Russia at that time was at the peak of its 'Wild East' chaos in the aftermath of the collapse of the Soviet Union. As we were to discover during the long and eventful couple of days there, pretty much anything went and everything was up for grabs. Extreme hedonism raged in the bars and clubs while the mafia clans waged wars on the street. Their battles were so bad that mothers often told their kids not to play near parked Mercedes because they had a nasty habit of exploding when the owner got in them.

I got a more prosaic insight into the anarchic state of Russia while waiting to board my Aeroflot flight at Dubai airport. The queue ground to a halt while a couple at the front argued for their right to carry eight car tyres, four televisions and a pair of stereo systems with them to the depleted new Russia as hand luggage. When they emerged triumphant from behind the mountain of cardboard boxes, I saw that they were the pilot and chief stewardess.

Aeroflot's liberal definition of hand luggage created a further challenge once on board the plane. Numerous boxes were piled high in the aisles at the rear of the aircraft and visiting the toilet involved clambering over a seven foot high stack of Sonys before jumping off the other side. The spectacularly grumpy stewardesses showed little interest in doing anything apart from protecting their own shopping. The flight was full and there had been all manner of mix-ups in the seat allocations. The staff absented themselves from the heated arguments that were going on all over the plane as it taxied down the runway. Several passengers were still standing and staggering around the aisle as it took off.

Once landed, I arrived at the front of the passport queue at Moscow's Sheremetyevo airport just in time to see my good friend and host, Steve Lyster, being led away by the local constabulary. I arrived in the evening, the last of our group to get there, whereas they had headed out for a spot of early sightseeing which had started with breakfast in a bar around the corner from Steve's flat and gone no further. By the time he came to pick me up, Steve was in a shambolic state. His dress sense was often just a few drinks away from dosshouse chic and he had fallen asleep on a bench in the arrivals hall. This led to him being arrested for vagrancy whilst I watched, stranded, from the wrong side of the passport counter. Fortunately, my concerns about how I was supposed to get into central Moscow or find out where I was supposed to be going, this being the pre-internet and mobile phone era, were quickly alleviated as his long-suffering girlfriend, Nicole, emerged from the car park having followed him. After collecting me, she then managed to secure his release by flashing her diplomatic pass and playing on the traditional Russian respect for the inebriated.

Little further can be said about that long weekend without jeopardising the security clearances of several good friends who are still working for the Foreign Office. Perhaps the only recollections fit for print are of insane nightclubs hidden in the basements of distant tower blocks; turning around to find my kid brother sitting atop the giant, white bust of Lenin that formed the centrepiece of one circular bar conducting a drink-scattering conga of scantily clad women along the counter; and breaking the Moscow all-comers record of ten passengers in a Lada taxi. Suffice to say, I returned to Dubai on the Tuesday morning with a throbbing mental note never to drink dodgy vodka sold by street kiosk vendors in recycled yoghurt pots again and to look out for Moscow as a potential posting destination.

By the time the opportunity for that posting arose several years later, I was a grown-up husband and father and firmly retired from carousing. But even, perhaps especially, for a sensible diplomat, Moscow remained about as good as overseas postings get.

On our first weekend there, and by now accompanied by our baby son, we stuck to our tried and trusted method of getting to know a new city by taking a walk. We had been invited to lunch by an old friend from our Tashkent days at an Uzbek restaurant. According to the map, it was only a couple of miles, at most, away from our temporary flat by the Moscow River.

It quickly became apparent that central Moscow would never be a place that many people walked around for pleasure. It was only October but a freezing wind was already howling as we crossed the Kutusovsky Bridge. Even without it, you could not hear yourself speak because of the traffic roaring alongside you and the clanking of the dilapidated trolleybuses.

A little further on, we turned onto the Garden Ring, which is perhaps the world's most inappropriately named street. To the uninitiated, it conjures up images of a shady, tree-lined boulevard made for strolling. In reality, the only green visible is on the traffic lights because it is an immense wall of concrete buildings alongside eight lanes of motorised mayhem. As I was soon to discover as a driver, the only rule of the road that matters in Moscow is do not hit anything, otherwise anything goes. Once behind the wheel, I found this approach rather liberating but as a pram-pusher trying to get across the road for some respite from the petrol fumes - emissions standards being something that had not reached Moscow yet - it was less than ideal. We eventually found a high footbridge, which was the only crossing point for miles around. As the two of us struggled to get the pram up the icy, steep stairs and over the bridge, we silently concluded that we would not be walking home after lunch or doing this again for a while.

Our stroll confirmed my earlier impressions about Moscow. This was a city that, at least for the past century, had been built to intimidate. Apart from in a few, small, older areas such as Patriarch's Ponds and along the old Arbat, every building seemed to be a colossal stone or concrete structure. And in a vast city of twelve million people, there were plenty of them. The totalitarian Soviet regime had created a city in its own image, looming oppressively over the man in the street and reminding him of his miniscule insignificance at every turn.

The air is reinforced by the Muscovites themselves. Out in the street, they can be rude and ruthless, happy to let the heavy wooden metro station doors slam in your face whilst pushing in front of you. Once you become accustomed to it, though, the exaggerated misanthropy ceases to feel offensive and starts to become comical. An early acquaintance of ours had us in stitches when she appeared flustered one morning and told us, with an entirely straight face, the shocking tale of the traveller who smiled at her on the metro. Apparently a young woman had been trying to attract her attention throughout the long ride into work by smiling and waving gently from along the packed carriage. As is the middle-aged Muscovite matriarch's wont, our acquaintance responded by glowering stonily at the young girl. When they both got off at the same stop, the young woman began to approach the older one, who finally cracked by demanding: 'why the hell are you smiling at me?' To which the youngster replied: 'because I am your God-daughter, Auntie Galina'.

In fairness, they had not seen each other for a few years and the young women had grown up a bit. But, rather than laugh at her mistake, Galina then stoked our hilarity further by launching into a spirited rant about how much energy she would waste if she went around smiling at everybody on the metro and that doing so would make them think she was simple.

The outward rudeness is just one illustration of how Moscow, and Russia in general, is a mass of contradictions. The language has a substantial vocabulary designed to permit great precision of meaning. One basic example is the sharp distinction made between a droog (friend), pryatel (mate) and znakomi (acquaintance). Among the unknown people out on the streets, it is every man, woman and babushka for themselves. But once you have passed through the znakomi stage, which brings a modest amount of formal respect, or at least less minor violence, and progressed to becoming a full-blown droog, then matters change dramatically.

Russians do not operate a shallow, pseudo-Facebook system whereby anyone you have ever had contact with qualifies as a friend. Becoming a droog conveys genuine status and it is conferred for life. It gets you behind both the concrete façade of people's homes and the stony face of their public persona. At this point you will discover that the same person who would happily push aggressively in front of you in a queue when they did not know you, will now willingly lay down their last kopeck or fight to their dying breath in order to help you.

Apart from the initial frostiness of the place and people, having arrived in October we soon had to get used to the all too long Moscow winter. I remembered Hull Docks as being a bit nippy at six o'clock on a January morning. But that was nothing compared to slithering across the Kutusovsky Bridge in sideways snow at minus 20 degrees centigrade, whilst occasionally glancing down to register that the mighty Moscow River had frozen solid in mid-ripple.

The coldest it got down to during our time there was thirty-nine below. That kind of temperature is a fascinating experience, albeit not for long. As soon as you step outside you feel a strange crackling sensation inside your nostrils as all of the moisture in them freezes on contact with the first air inhaled. Then your face starts to hurt, your eyeballs begin to ache and it rapidly stops being fun anymore.

Once, in such temperatures, a friend of mine came straight down to a hotel lobby after showering and realised that he had left his woolly hat in his room. Given that he was only going to the bar across the street, he decided to make a run for it. As soon as he stepped outside, he felt the hair on his head spike up solid and an instant headache. Within seconds, the hefty hotel doorman grabbed him by the shoulders, dragged him to the kitchens and shoved his head into the warm oven. The doorman explained that this rough treatment was actually a mercy mission – apparently freezing your head in this way can rapidly cause brain damage.

Moscow also provided me with a coldest I have ever been at a sporting event story, that I will one day enjoy boring my grandchildren with. I am sure they will find it a nice change from the one about me catching hypothermia watching Hull FC away at Thrum Hall, Halifax in the long lost days when rugby league was played in winter. It was a Europa League quarter-final between Lokomotiv Moscow and Sevilla of Spain. Apparently UEFA has a rule that games have to be called off on player safety grounds if the temperature is below minus 15 degrees centigrade. On this occasion, it was bang on that when the decision to play was taken at midday. By the 8:30pm kick-off time, it was considerably colder and the mercury descended further as the match went on. I am rarely impressed by modern footballers but I was bowled over by how Sevilla – a team from the hottest city in Europe - coped with the conditions that night. It probably helped that rolling about in feigned agony on the floor was off the agenda because anyone trying it would have got stuck frozen to the ice on impact. But even so, Sevilla got on with their business uncomplainingly and won 1-0. It was pretty obvious at that point that they would go on to win the tournament, which they did at a canter.

Up in the stands, my mate and I only barely managed to survive to the final whistle by conducting a non-stop ninety minute relay to the tea stand for hot drinks. The experience was proof of the power of childhood conditioning. Once, as a five year old, I had been bursting for the toilet towards the end of a Hull City–Chelsea game and caused my Uncle Les to miss two last minute goals. He made me swear never to leave a game early again and even that freezing night at Lokomotiv could not make me break my promise.

A further challenge posed by the extreme winter conditions was taking a baby-cum-toddler who did not like being cooped up inside for long periods outside for a walk and play. The system we had for him, and, subsequently, our first daughter, who was born in Moscow, was to lay them on the floor and dress them in multiple layers, topped off with a thick sheepskin all-in-one suit that left them mummified and immobile. Every time you went indoors, such as into a shop, café or someone's home, all of these layers had to be peeled off again quickly because Moscow buildings in winter are invariably heated to tropical summer temperatures. This could mean a temperature swing of 50 degrees centigrade as soon as you crossed the threshold and result in your child turning from frozen bundle to melted puddle in ten seconds flat.

The reason for this was that all but the newest Moscow buildings are on the same centrally controlled, city-wide central heating system. The system is switched on by the local authorities on the first day of winter - which in Russian terms is an official date on the calendar in mid-October, not a fluid concept based on the prevailing weather conditions - and off on the first day of spring. This extreme form of literal central heating leads to the environmentally horrifying spectacle of walking around Moscow in sub-zero weather and seeing many of the windows open to let some of the stifling internal heat out.

Another common practice that you quickly get used to in the Moscow winter is wearing big boots to get from one place to another and carrying a pair of regular shoes with you to change into when you get there. The only people who don't are some of the stylishly turned out Muscovite women. Although the city authorities do an admirable job of clearing the vast quantities of snow and ice from the road, it is impossible to keep up entirely and the paths are generally less well serviced. This means that you often find yourself walking on thick sheets of ice, which I found treacherous even in heavy-soled walking boots. Some of the local women, in contrast, manage to float elegantly across the top of it in fashionable high-heels with no hint of a slide or cautious step.

Even after the last snowfall of the winter and the temperature has risen well above zero, it takes weeks for the enormous mountains of grubby cleared snow by the roadsides to melt. The slow thaw leads to the grisly annual Moscow phenomenon of dozens of dead bodies emerging from the melting piles. These poor souls are almost always drunks who have been lulled to sleep by the combination of alcohol and extreme cold and been quickly buried by the falling snow. With typical ultra-dark humour, Russians refer to these victims as snowdrops because their emergence to the surface signals the arrival of spring.

In short, Moscow is a tough town, especially during the harsh winter. But, in keeping with its status as the capital of contradictions, it contains great beauty too. The city never looks better than on a crisp winter day with a piercingly sharp blue sky and a fresh covering of snow. My first visit to the Kremlin, Red Square and Lenin's tomb came on one such occasion. I had grown-up watching May Day parades of the

Soviet Union's military might across the Square. Finding myself standing, as a Moscow resident and accredited British diplomat no less, amid the unmistakeable, vividly colourful onion domes of St Basil's Cathedral and the red contours of the Kremlin whilst visualising the ghost of Brezhnev saluting the soldiery from the top of the mausoleum was one of those breathtaking 'how on earth did I get here' moments that were one of the joys of being in the Diplomatic Service.

Those sentiments were a regular feature of life in Moscow. It is impossible for a Cold War kid who is absorbed by history and international politics not to get a kick out of visiting the Kremlin, the huge Great Patriotic War memorial at Victory Park, as the Russians call World War II or the fading ghosts of Soviet glories at the VDNKh exhibition centre, with its pavilions dedicated to the Cosmanaut programme and the glorious achievements of the USSR.

The thrill was a constant feature of everyday life too, as I travelled to meetings in the Stalin-era skyscrapers of the Foreign Ministry or Moscow State University on the Moscow Metro with its long, rapid escalators to the exquisitely marbled, muraled and chandeliered stations deep underground. It was there in the Cyrillic signage and gigantic modern neon billboards everywhere. As well as having an incredible history, Russia also has a deep culture. In summer we would stroll around Gorky Park, the setting for the eponymous film that I have always loved. In winter, we sledged and staged Sunday morning snowball fights in the grounds of the beautiful Orthodox Novodevichy Monastery, where many great Russian writers and composers are buried. Or we bought wonderful fresh bread in a shop around the corner from Patriarch's Ponds, the setting for Bulgakov's great novel *The Master and Margerita*, where the kids played in the park.

The Accidental Diplomat

Bulgakov's story courageously satirised Soviet society under Stalin using the cover of magic realism and characters disguised as creatures. Animal-related surrealism lingered in Moscow life in the late 2000s too. One morning we awoke to the news that we should watch out for drunken elephants on the loose from the nearby Moscow zoo. The zookeepers' plan to ward off the winter cold by supplying the elephants with buckets of vodka had backfired when the beasts became boisterous and trashed their enclosure, Keith Moon style.

We were equally alarmed a few weeks later to find someone dressed as Superman attempting to restrain an elephant that was standing on our street. Fortunately, we soon discovered this one was merely experiencing a bun-fuelled sugar rush after an oligarch had hired it and the man in the costume to entertain at his kid's birthday party in the notorious restaurant a few doors down from the Embassy patronised by the Novy Russky, the new-rich.

The one unexpected animal mystery that I never got to the bottom of came almost every week when I went to watch the weekend rugby league on TV. There was already something odd about strolling down the Soviet showpiece avenue of the Novy Arbat, past the glittering gangsters' hangout on the corner with their Porsches, Mercedes and Ferraris parked outside guarded by beefed-up, black-suited bodyguards and into the basement of the Metallitsa casino to see some Super League on their bootleg Sky satellite system.

After slipping between the Chinese businessmen and heavily jewelled Georgians gambling at the roulette tables, I would enter the enclave in the back room to be greeted by my friends Cumbrian Martin, Dan from Huddersfield and, for a time, sundry St. Helensians who were setting up the new Pilkington glass factory in Moscow.It was like our own off-kilter Working Men's club. But the greater incongruity came when I left to walk home in the early hours of the morning. Whatever the weather, I would always be passed on the broad pavement by two ladies immaculately turned out in full riding gear atop a pair of thoroughbred horses.

Where they came from, I never discovered because there was nothing but colossal concrete buildings, thirty metre high billboards and tarmac for many miles around. Nor did I ever see them at any other time of the day. In previous times I would have blamed the booze and an imagination over-fertilised by too many European art-house movies. But, by this time, with a busy job and a young family, I was barely indulging in either and never failed to be baffled by the thought of that sight. Perhaps they were members of the world's first urban fox hunt.

Whatever they were up to, I should probably have not been so surprised to see them riding through the city at two in the morning because Moscow often felt like a place where anything was possible, if you had the money to pay for it. In less than two decades, the city had gone from being the capital of communism and chronic scarcity to capitalism on steroids. By the mid-2000s, it had a New York 24/7 feel to it with everything being available, all of the time. The common street scene had changed from old ladies queuing for bread to the new-monied set swanning into sushi bars. But, the dark side, was that many of the apparent new achievers were fake, with much of their wealth being acquired by shady dealings and dodgy shortcuts.

It may have been a mutant form of capitalism but it had taken a firm grip on Moscow. I was always struck by the symbolism of the memorial close to Sheremetyevo Airport which consisted of two large tank traps and marked the most advanced point the Nazis had reached during World War II. When I first visited Moscow on that early-1990s Easter weekend the memorial stood in splendid isolation on empty land a few miles from the city boundary. By the time I came back to Russia to live in 2005, it had been engulfed by IKEAs, gaudy car dealerships and a forest of huge neon-lit advertising hoardings. The capitalists had clearly succeeded where Hitler had failed and taken Moscow.

21. The Russia House

IN keeping with the character of the place, our own living experience spanned the old and new Moscow. We spent our first five months staying in the dour old diplomatic blocks, an immense apartment complex where foreign diplomats and journalists had been compulsorily corralled in Soviet times in order to make it easier for the KGB to keep an eye on them, before we were eventually allocated a flat on the Embassy compound across the river. This was an improvement for my wife, as most things in the city were more easily accessible from there. I was also delighted at no longer having to slide and stumble across the freezing bridge every morning and evening.

We had some initial misgivings about moving onto the compound because we feared it would feel like living in a gilded ghetto, isolated from the country we had come to live in. There was also the concern that many other colleagues voiced about living in what was, in effect, a small goldfish bowl of a British diplomatic village sealed in the heart of a major city. In fact, we quickly realised, that there was a simple solution to such problems – you could just go out through the front door and into Russia whenever you felt claustrophobic.

The Accidental Diplomat

The British Embassy compound had only been completed a few years earlier. It had been designed in a rare fit of government extravagance and optimism about a new, prosperous relationship with Russia following the fall of the Soviet Union. The Foreign Office has never been as lavishly funded as the *Daily Express* would have you believe - we do not mainline gin and tonic twenty four hours a day and many of our fancier Embassy buildings are ancient historical inheritances or gifts of foreign governments that cost minimal rent.

The Embassy is a modern building out of character with the Soviet monoliths alongside it on the Smolenskaya Embankment. Consequently, its appearance divides opinion. The then Mayor of Moscow, Yuri Luzhkov, something of a Soviet monolith himself, rarely missed an opportunity to point out volubly how much he hated it. Luzhkov knew something about buildings too. He once memorably told, with a straight face, a visiting British business delegation hosted by the Embassy that their suggestion that Moscow was inhospitable to small and medium-sized enterprises was wrong because his wife, Yelena Baturina, had started a small business and turned it into the biggest construction company in Russia, if not the world. Clearly, this multi-billion rouble success story was all down to the nurturing business environment of Moscow and Baturina's entrepreneurial genius. Being married to the notoriously corrupt man who signed most of the contracts and planning permissions had absolutely nothing to do with it.

To be fair to Luzhkov, the Embassy building is not that attractive from the outside, although claiming that it spoiled the look of that part of Moscow was a stretch – akin to claiming that putting lipstick on a warthog makes it look ugly. The real attractions are on the inside. The complex is made up of four main buildings, three residential and one containing the offices. It was a pleasurable commute to my desk involving two lift rides and a twenty-yard stroll down a warm, red-carpeted corridor. The complex has a bar, gym, swimming pool, squash and tennis courts. In contrast to the heavy structures that dominated in Moscow, it is light, bright and airy. Best of all, the flats are well-designed and comfortable. The design also alleviates the risks associated with living exclusively among your work colleagues. There are only two flats on each floor of the residential blocks, none of which overlook each other, thus offering a degree of privacy.

One of the most attractive features of ours was its two large balconies, an open air one for the summer and a closed in one with double-glazing. The open balcony was more aesthetically pleasing than practical because the noise and grime from the Moscow streets rendered it unusable. But the enclosed one provided a perfect play area for our son and we spent hours gazing from it at the spectacular views of the river and cityscape. I was also fascinated to discover that, well-built though the building was, when the temperature went below minus 20 degrees centigrade, the windows still froze up on the inside.

The enclosed balcony later acquired a new occupant when our first daughter was born. Most Embassy staff usually went back to the UK or their home countries, in the case of foreign-born wives, to deliver their babies. A complicated pregnancy meant that this was not an option for us, so we fell back on the excellent care and facilities offered by the new Moscow Perinatal Centre. The only problem was that, due to the vastness of Moscow and its chronic traffic problems, every journey to there could take up to two hours each way. By the time the delivery came, I had memorised the locations of all of the cafes and restaurants en-route from which hot water might be obtained and established a contingency plan for delivering a baby in the back of a Peugeot 307 whilst stuck at traffic lights in Moscow's Yugo-Zapadnaya district.

Thankfully, our daughter arrived late in the evening, when the traffic was lighter and my back-up plan was not needed. The only hitch came when I collected my wife and child from the hospital to go home. We were led to room next to the exit to wait, so we thought, our signing-out papers. In fact, we were being prepared for a Russian practice that should have been apparent from the pitying glances we were receiving from the other families, who were all dressed to the nines as if for a wedding and carrying armfuls of flowers. It turned out that the rather nice norm is to have a short party with champagne and cake to mark the family's departure for home, with the event being videoed for posterity. In our sorry case, the film we were presented with by the hospital shows our new baby being accompanied by two weary, dishevelled, parents in scruffy tracksuits and a small, fading four day old bouquet salvaged from the hospital room.

As we should have anticipated after having already lived there for a couple of years, you get filmed a lot as a British diplomat in Moscow, whether you like it or not.

The whiff of espionage is ever-present when working as an envoy to Russia. Our Embassy there is in the highest security category, which means the building and those working in it are subject to a panoply of security restrictions. Some of these secret measures might ring bells with spy fiction fans and they certainly create an exciting cloak-and-dagger atmosphere around going to work.

The intensive precautions are also absolutely necessary in Moscow. The security services are influential in many countries but Russia under Vladimir Putin is a state that is actually run by KGB officers. Worse still, they have combined their unreconstructed secret policeman's outlook with the practices of the mafia to seemingly acquire vast wealth for themselves and create an oppressive regime under which to live.

President Putin once described the fall of the Soviet Union as: 'The greatest geopolitical catastrophe of the last century' and makes no secret of his nostalgia for the days when KGB men like him first ruled the roost. Before being despatched to the backwater of Dresden in then East Germany, Putin's KGB job was to spy and conduct petty harassment on foreigners and dissidents in his home town of St Petersburg. It is no surprise, then, that his subsequent rise to political power has been accompanied by a return to some of the old ways by its successor, the Federal Security Service.

UK-Russia relations were strained during my time in Moscow. Putin saw us as the hated USA's closest ally and the most difficult European country to push around regarding his alleged human rights abuses and bullying of neighbouring states. Most of all, he was infuriated by the British courts granting political asylum to opponents such as the oligarch Boris Berezovsky and the Chechen leader, Ahmed Zakayev, against both of whom he had an intense personal vendetta.

This meant that our Embassy staff were subjected to a campaign of harassment reminiscent of the darkest Cold War days. The Ambassador and his wife were targeted extensively by Putin's organisation Nashi, meaning ours, as in one of ours. As part of a relentless campaign of threatening behaviour, they were regularly jostled and had their car attacked by large groups of Nashi thugs when they went out.

At the other end of the scale, our locally recruited

Russian staff had it even worse. Unlike accredited British diplomats, they could not leave Russia after a three year posting nor did they have diplomatic immunity to protect them against the authorities. Despite this pressure, some of them refused to do the FSB's bidding by spying on their colleagues or passing on information acquired from within the Embassy. As a consequence, some of our Russian work mates were denied permission to travel outside the country, had their children threatened with physical harm and were told that their elderly, sick parents would be refused necessary medical treatment.

For those of us in the middle ranks, the sinister security facts of life in Moscow were just something you had to get used to. We had to assume that our phone, apartment and cars were bugged, private e-mails read and internet use monitored. Cameras tracked our movements in and out of the Embassy compound, where many of us also lived. I was reliably informed that I was followed around the streets when going about my daily life.

This tight monitoring led to some of my colleagues making an unfortunate surprise appearance one evening on Russian State TV's equivalent of *Panorama*. The grainy footage showed them kicking a rock late one night in a Moscow park. Rather than drunken tomfoolery, it was alleged that they were repairing a concealed transmitter using methods that were more Austin Powers than James Bond.

Apart from information gathering, the aim of the FSB's surveillance of us was to instil a feeling of unease and paranoia. Personally, I found it surprisingly easy to adapt to the constant eavesdropping and rarely worried about it. I quickly learned to be circumspect when talking about any aspect of work outside the secure zone of the Embassy building and to keep personal gossip to a minimum. Such restraint was necessary because the FSB is notoriously adept at using any personal weaknesses and secrets it picks up on for blackmail purposes.

Ultimately, these enforced inhibitions were more frustrating for my wife than I. Her claustrophobic feeling of living in an ivory tower was exacerbated by my giving her an even more taciturn and bland account than usual of what I was up to all day and the foibles of my Embassy colleagues.

I soon got used to being followed by cameras and in person too. By this time, I was living an entirely virtuous and blameless family life, so whoever got landed with my case file at FSB HQ must have had a very dull professional existence indeed. In fact, the feeling that I was a character in a le Carré novel added welcome spice to my strolls to the supermarket or to watch the rugby league in the Metallitsa Sports Bar.

The direct personal impact of the FSB's activities on our non-Embassy friends was rather more troubling. One Camerounian, who had lived in Russia since he was a student and had a Russian family and passport, was regularly followed after visiting us at home. He was taken in several times for questioning by the FSB, who grilled him about our relationship and dropped menacing hints about his well-being and livelihood to pressure him into providing them with regular information about us.

The FSB went further with Freddie, the very nice Philippino we employed early in our time in Moscow to clean, iron and babysit for our young son. One morning, when we were away on holiday, he called us. He had been picked up and held incognito by the secret police. They treated him roughly and told him worse would follow if he did not agree to spy on us and use his access to the Embassy to perform other acts of espionage for them.

Freddie was too decent to do anything of the sort. Instead, terrified and unable to call on us for help because we were out of the country, he went straight home from FSB custody, packed all of the belongings he could carry, put together just enough money from his savings and urgent loans from friends to buy a ticket on the first available flight and left the country he had lived in for a decade, never to return. This was a traumatic experience for him, not least because he had relatives at home depending on the wages he was able to send them.

Even if the most significant effects were on those around us, there were occasions when my carefully cultivated air of insouciance about the surveillance slipped and I succumbed to the paranoia that can result from living in the peculiar circumstances of the British Embassy in Moscow.

One such occasion arose when I could not find my passport in its usual place in the bedside drawer. It was well-known that FSB operatives sometimes entered Embassy staff accommodation to mess around with things in order to inflict psychological stress on the person concerned. After turning our flat upside down in an unsuccessful search, I concluded that FSB intrusion must be the explanation for it and duly reported the matter to our Chief Security Officer. He was sceptical because passport-stealing was not a trademarked tactic, they tended to go in more for things like emptying perfume bottles, turning your fridge off and crapping in your toilet and not flushing it. But the CSO sympathetically recorded my incident report anyway.

Several weeks after I had put our Vice-Consul to the bother of issuing a new passport, my wife found the old one in one of her handbags - having repeatedly sworn blind that she could not possibly have it. It had been there since a weekend trip we had made to Lithuania a couple of months earlier. It is fair to say that I felt a fool when I presented the now-cancelled passport to the Chief Security Officer and Vice-Consul in order to close the case. It was a trivial comedy of errors but at the other end of the scale, having a major state run by a secret regime has had deadly consequences for many people.

One ugly case that I became closely involved in was that of Alexander Litvinenko, a former FSB anti-organised crime officer who had upset some powerful people in Russia by revealing high-level corruption before escaping to the UK. It turned out not to be far enough away. His murder hit the headlines all over the world and dominated my last few months in Moscow.

The basic facts of the case have been well-documented by the media. On 1 November, 2006 Litvinenko fell seriously ill with a mystery complaint and was hospitalised in London. His agonising death eventually came three weeks later, with his slow deterioration being broadcast daily around the world via TV pictures. The mystery cause was identified just hours before he died, when it was discovered that he had been poisoned with a rare variety of a radioactive substance called polonium-210.

Suspicion quickly fell upon a meeting Litvinenko had had with two business contacts and supposedly former KGB agents, Andrei Lugovoi and Dmitry Kovtun, in the bar at London's Millenium Hotel earlier in the day on which he had fallen ill. The Russian authorities rapidly made it clear that there was no possibility of the two main suspects being extradited from Russia to the UK to face trial. Indeed, Putin's governing party later appointed Lugovoi as an MP in the Russian parliament, a post which confers immunity from criminal prosecution.

I was included in the small team formed by the

Embassy to handle the affair. For all that the murder was sickening, I have to admit that from a selfish point of view being involved the investigation was one of the most exciting times of my professional life. Aside from the dramatic facts of the case, the search for radioactive evidence and pursuit of the suspects brought me into contact with a fascinating array of hi-tech equipment and characters that were entirely in keeping with the classics of the spy fiction genre, together with a touch of *The Sweeney*.

Once they had finished their main investigation in London, a crack Metropolitan Police Special Branch team came out to Moscow for several weeks to pursue the case further. I was responsible for setting up their incident room in a quiet corner of the Embassy and for helping them during their stay. Some of the foot soldiers in the Met team could easily have been the direct descendants of Carter and Regan. They were not people you would want to be locked in an interview room with when you had got on their wrong side. But I found their sharp, raw wit great to be around and the comic relief they often brought to a serious situation started from the moment they arrived in Moscow.

We had tried to arrange a quiet arrival for the Met team but the Russian state-controlled media were predictably out in force to greet them at the airport. This inadvertently helped me out because I was there to meet some other visitors involved in the investigation off the same flight and was able to slip them through unnoticed, thanks to the distraction created by the scrum around the police. As I was on my way through the arrivals hall, I passed one of the more gnarled looking coppers, a huge bloke in his late-thirties, as his post-flight cigarette was disrupted by a TV camera being shoved in his face. With a smile conveying humour and menace in equal proportions, he told the cameraman in a sardonic

Cockney voice: 'Please don't point that thing at me, son – my mum doesn't know I smoke'.

The squad were a fascinating and impressive bunch to observe at work. The two commanding officers were hard-nosed but had a veneer of diplomatic smoothness that allowed them to work well with our senior Embassy staff. It also enabled them to keep their cool with the senior Russian officials such as the Prosecutor-General, whose permission they needed to do almost anything on his patch. Their self-control was admirable because it must have been frustrating to realise quite quickly that the case would be extremely difficult to conclude, given the Russians refusal to contemplate extraditing the chief suspects. The investigation remains open.

22. Smiley People

ASIDE from the lingering spy novel undertones, the Political Section of the Embassy in Moscow is one of the most interesting and exciting places in the world to work as a British diplomat.

For all of its problems, Russia is still a big, important country. It is also professionally challenging because we frequently disagree with the Russians about issues of major global importance. Another conundrum is that despite having, proportionately, perhaps more hyper-intelligent and hard-working people than any other country on earth – including many of the Foreign Ministry officials I dealt with, it has staggered throughout history from one incompetent, corrupt and brutal government to another.

My job title in Moscow was 2nd Secretary Political (External). This involved monitoring, reporting on and attempting to influence Russian foreign policy across a vast swathe of the world, including Africa, Asia, the Middle East and Latin America. I also covered global issues such as drugs policy, arms control and international human rights matters. The main impetus for this work was the status of the UK and Russia as permanent members of the United Nations Security

Council. Not much happens on global political issues without the approval of the Security Council and its five permanent members; the others are the US, France and China. They are the only countries with the individual power to veto any decisions it takes.

In practice, much of my time was spent trooping backwards and forwards to the imposing, Stalinist Foreign Ministry building for meetings with my Russian counterparts. The idea was to increase our understanding of their opinions and policies on specific global issues and persuade them of the merits of ours. Much of this work is the basic bread and butter of diplomacy. It is the unseen, painstaking negotiation that leads to crises being mitigated or, perhaps most importantly and invisibly, prevented from happening in the first place. To someone with my interests, being involved in high stakes, high profile matters of crucial world importance such as participating in the negotiations on Iran's nuclear weapons' programme was an experience to treasure.

The only slight downside is that the success or otherwise of it is often hard to quantify. The best outcomes are often the issues that did not arise because of the understanding and cooperation built up over a long period of time. As a cog in a big worldwide wheel, it can be almost impossible to assess what part your efforts played in preventing something potentially catastrophic when you cannot be sure it would ever have happened anyway. The only thing certain is that an already dangerous world would be a whole lot more violent and unstable without the constant ongoing churn of discreet diplomacy.

There are occasional golden moments, though, when you know for sure that you have done something that made a real global difference. One such during my time in Moscow was the transfer to the international Special Court for Sierra Leone of Charles Taylor, the brutal former Liberian President and warlord.

During the Sierra Leonean civil war, Taylor, as President of neighbouring Liberia, had trained, directed and supported with cash and weapons the crazed rebel forces who murdered and cold-bloodedly mutilated thousands of Sierra Leoneans, partly through recruiting, drugging and brainwashing large numbers of child soldiers. Taylor's principle objective was to gain control of Sierra Leone's diamond mines for his own enrichment. The war there was ended and democratic government restored, thanks in large part to an UN-backed British military intervention to rout the rebels. Taylor was deposed by his domestic opponents in Liberia but had found sanctuary in Nigeria, from where he continued to foment violence and instability in his homeland and neighbouring countries.

He was indicted for war crimes by the SCSL and eventually arrested by the Nigerians. But one of the problems was the difficulty of ensuring adequate security for his trial in the West African region, where many of his men were still armed and at large. In order to get around this, a plan was hatched to conduct it under the auspices of the SCSL but using the facilities of the International Courts in The Hague.

Unfortunately, the Russians had so far blocked this proposal at the Security Council. They routinely obstruct any plan to take action against war crimes or enforce justice against the perpetrators. Their official argument is that the long-established international principle of non-interference in the domestic affairs of a state should be sacrosanct. A cynic, and, after years of close-up experience of watching them in action, I am one, would say that the reason they are allergic to international justice is to avoid precedents being set. The current Russian government is keen to preserve its freedom to persecute its own citizens without outside interference or fear of future prosecution.

I met my counterparts in the Russian Foreign Ministry on the day the vote on the Resolution to send Taylor to trial in The Hague was due to take place in New York which was during the night in Moscow, due to the time difference. With more passion and force than usual, I deployed the arguments that my colleagues at our Mission to the UN in New York, the Foreign Office in London and I had developed in an attempt to convince the Russians that the Resolution was tightly worded in such a way that it could only be applied to the Taylor case without setting any future landmark. The Russians were non-committal but promised politely, as usual, to consider my points. I was therefore delighted to find, when I came in to work the next morning, a telegram from New York offering personal congratulations for persuading the Russians to change their vote to permit the transfer of Taylor to The Hague for trial. It was highly unusual to be sent such a message in the internal Diplomatic Service correspondence system.

Taylor was subsequently sentenced to fifty years imprisonment for his crimes and although still poor and precarious, Sierra Leone and Liberia have been at peace for a decade. Their chances of remaining so are greatly enhanced by the removal of Taylor from the scene. There are few jobs in the world that enable an ordinary lad from Hull to feel the satisfaction of making such a positive contribution to so many peoples' lives.

Part of the reason for success in this example, I believe, goes beyond the quality of the arguments I was able to make about a foreign policy issue. There was also the human factor built up over years of engagement on numerous issues with the Russian counterparts who were handling the case. While I have never just gone through the motions of reading out the script I had been given by the Foreign Office - with the possible exception of the time when I was sent to lobby the Foreign Ministry about the Iraq war, using lines I did not believe in, let alone expect the Russians to swallow - human nature means that there are inevitably issues on which your personal views enable you to speak more persuasively. The Taylor case was one such example. Because they knew me as a straightforward and respected diplomatic colleague, my Russian opposite numbers recognised the honesty and strength of my arguments and genuine efforts to accommodate their concerns in the action we proposed should be taken.

For my part, despite my scepticism about the cynical policies their government often required them to adopt, I had the utmost respect for my Russian colleagues. While the nature of the Russia-UK political relationship and the security restrictions their authorities placed on interaction with foreign diplomats was always going to make real personal friendships difficult to form beyond work, many of them were genuinely warm, friendly and humorous. I respected them even more when they remained so during the tense period in relations that followed the Litvinenko murder.

My Russian opposite numbers' knowledge of their subjects was frequently impressive and even daunting. This made debating and negotiating with them a compelling professional challenge. In contrast with the British system, whereby many officers, like me, deal with a wide range of issues during our careers, the Russians often specialise in one subject for their whole working lives. This contrast came to the fore most on highly technical issues such as arms control. As someone new to the subject, who did not know what a

MANPAD was or which way to point one, it was a real stretch to hold my own with an opposite number who knew the details going back decades of the negotiations on treaties to limit the proliferation of different types of weapons.

Aside from the bread and butter business of discussing the intricacies of issues like the Middle East peace process and international arms control treaties with the Foreign Ministry, my job in Moscow opened up the way to meeting some fascinating people. One vehicle for this was when the UK held the presidency of the G8 grouping of the world's most powerful countries during my first year there. Among many other things, the presidency involves hosting the leaders' summit and setting its priorities for the year. One of the two chosen by Prime Minister Blair was African development. To this end, he created and chaired a Commission for Africa consisting of eminent persons from around the world such as Bob Geldof and the then Ethiopian President, Meles Zenawi.

The Commission wrote an impressive report which made a number of recommendations on how the rest of the world could assist in Africa's democratic and economic development. I was put in charge of promoting this initiative in Russia and convincing the Russians to support the recommendations.

Russia had faced all manner of difficulties of its own since the collapse of the Soviet Union and its worldview had shrunk as a consequence. Nowhere was this more apparent than in Africa, where all of the links built up with the continent during the Cold War proxy struggle with the USA had withered away. Russia seemingly had few ongoing interests there and Africa was virtually invisible in the media. As a consequence, there were very few obvious opinion formers in the political, business and cultural worlds to attempt to influence. The task of promoting our G8 African priority was, then, one that would require some imagination.

One of the first people I approached with my ideas for a series of events to raise the profile of Africa and our initiatives was Yelena Hanga. She is a famous TV host in Russia and has the unusual distinction of being perhaps the best-known black Russian since the national poet, Pushkin. She, in turn, put me in touch with her mother, Lily Golden, who was an amazing woman with an incredible life story.

Lily's grandfather, Hilliard Golden was a freed slave who married a Native American and later became a landowner in Mississippi until he was chased out by the Ku Klux Klan, who repeatedly burnt down his home and crops. Her father, Oliver John Golden, was a communist and agricultural expert, who specialised in cotton growing techniques. He married a fellow communist, a Polish-Jewish New Yorker, Bertha Bialek, who was estranged from her family as a result. As anyone with a passing knowledge of American history will realise, a mixed Black/Native American/Jewish/Communist couple was not the easiest thing to be in early twentieth century United States. Their impressive collection of the most oppressed minority identities in the US encouraged Oliver and Bertha to emigrate to the Soviet Union, after a detour where Oliver enlisted in the French Army to fight in World War I. By 1931 they had settled in the Soviet Republic of Uzbekistan, where they were prime movers in setting up the cotton industry that became a mainstay of that Republic's economy for decades afterwards.

Lily was born in 1934 and raised in Tashkent. As well as being a champion Soviet tennis player, she became a renowned scholar who rose to become Director of the Institute of African Studies at Moscow State University, the country's paramount higher education institution, and, especially in her later years, a prominent civil rights and anti-racism activist. Lily was identified by the Soviet leadership as brilliant young woman and they regularly sought her advice. Her close contacts with the Kremlin leadership and nascent African revolutionary leaders led to her being branded by Western Cold War propaganda during the 1950's and '60's as the brains behind the Soviet policy of exporting communist revolution to Africa, although she always played down this accusation when I met her.

What certainly did happen along the way was that she married a Zanzibari politician called Kassim Hanga. He helped to mastermind a coup in Zanzibar in 1964 and its unification with Tanganyika to form the newly independent nation of Tanzania and became a government minister. Hanga's exalted position did not last long, though, because he soon became embroiled in a political dispute with some of his former comrades in arms and disappeared. Lily never saw him again and eventually discovered through her contacts, including Stalin's daughter, Svetlana Josefna, that he had been imprisoned and tortured before being shot through the head at close range and dumped in the Indian Ocean.

In her later years, after the fall of the Soviet Union, Lily was able to explore her American roots. She devoted a lot of time to promoting understanding between the US and Russia and, in particular, the anti-racism struggle. The latter work had become vital, and dangerous, in Russia following the rise of numerous, murderous gangs of far-right thugs and neo-fascist political parties.

Lily Golden was the twentieth century history of the world in one person – her life story encompassed slavery, the rise of communism, the Cold War, anti-colonialism and the fight against racism. On top of all that, she was a lovely, warm and witty woman whose stories could not only leave you spellbound but also in stitches.

She once told my wife and I about the time she had been sitting in a Moscow restaurant when a man came up to her and began, in a very friendly, familiar way asking all manner of questions about the health of her family and general life. She began responding, slightly embarrassed that she could not place someone who so clearly knew her well and yet seemed to be a complete stranger. Eventually, this began to feel ridiculous and she apologetically asked the man how they were acquainted. He replied that it was perfectly understandable that she did not know him but he had been the KGB officer who secretly spied on her movements, read her mail and listened in on her conversations for years.

Meeting people like Lily Golden is beyond anything I could have dreamed of, growing up. Nice houses in exotic foreign climes, access-all-areas diplomatic passes and an endless round of parties are often cited as the privileges of life as a diplomat. But for me such fripperies, enjoyable though they were, paled into insignificance when compared to the amazing honour it was sitting in Lily Golden's Moscow flat listening to her stories while she cooked lunch.

Not for the first time, I had that 'how did I get here' glow.

End

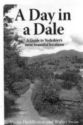
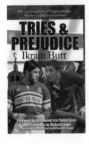

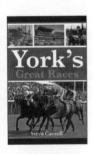

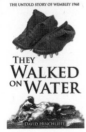

Just what *is* Yorkshireness...?

Yorkshire ... God's Own County ... The Broad Acres ... the Texas of England ... home to some of the UK's most captivating landscapes, coastlines, food, literature, history, music, tea, film, sport and beer, when Britain's largest county and its residents get you in their grip, you are unlikely to escape soon.

Venue for Le Grand Départ of 2014's Tour de France and voted the Leading Tourist Destination in Europe - beating off the challenges of Paris, Rome, London (ha!) and Vienna - the White Rose county is on the rise. *Slouching Towards Blubberhouses* is a timely and comical look at a region that is by turns friendly, uncompromising, boastful, blunt and maddeningly self-aware, from the viewpoint both of its chosen ones, who wouldn't live anywhere else, and those who look on in envy - or irritation - from outside.

It delves beneath the eeh bah gum clichés of whippets, clogs, flat caps and moth-eaten wallets to explore what really makes Tykes tick. And it wonders if coming from Yorkshire still means owt in a changing and diverse 21st century.

Slouching Towards Blubberhouses

- A (right grand) Tour de Yorkshireness

By Tony Hannan

Strike!

The Tour That Died of Shame

By John Coffey

The 1926-27 New Zealand 'All Blacks' tour of Great Britain was the most tempestuous sporting venture of all time. It led to seven of the players being disqualified for life on their return home.

Set against the backdrop of a financially crippling miners' strike, the 'guilty' tourists rebelled against their controversial coach, an Australian who himself was suspended for part of the tour by English authorities.

Nineteen loyal players were left to carry on bravely against overwhelming odds in the midst of a harsh English winter, some of them backing up for as many as fifteen consecutive matches.

Strike! The Tour That Died of Shame is that story.

It is a tale of hardship and heroism, courage and cover-up, examined in depth for the very first time. It is an investigation of what went wrong with a tour that promised so much. It seeks to establish who - if anyone - was really to blame. And it is a fascinating slice of sporting social history whose reverberations continue to be felt today.

www.scratchingshedpublishing.com

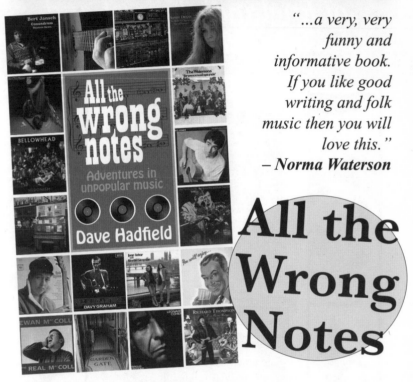

Adventures in Unpopular Music
By Dave Hadfield

For almost 50 years, Dave Hadfield has followed the genres of music that grabbed his youthful heart and mind. Now, in ALL THE WRONG NOTES, he has written not just a musical memoir, but a personal and social history of the last half-century. Like a Zelig with a finger in his ear, he has been where folk music has happened and describes it, affectionately but warts-and-all, in a way it has never been described before.

Hadfield's sure ear for quirks and eccentricities produces unique takes on major figures like Bob Dylan, Ewan MacColl and Leonard Cohen. It celebrates the foot-soldiers and their role in keeping left-field music alive. Humorous and provocative in equal measure, ALL THE WRONG NOTES is the key to a fascinating world of music.

THE STORY OF FOOTBALL:
via the Moors, Dales and Wolds of England's largest and proudest county

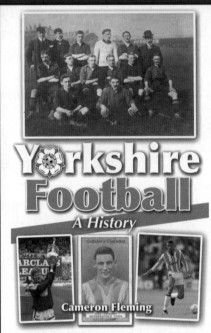

YORKSHIRE FOOTBALL - A HISTORY
 Cameron Fleming

ISBN: 978-0956252654

Scratching Shed Publishing Ltd

Funny Bones

My Life in Comedy

By Freddie 'Parrotface' Davies

with a foreword by **Ken Dodd**

Freddie Davies
Funny Bones

My Life in Comedy
An Autobiography with Anthony Teague
Foreword by Ken Dodd OBE

In 1964, a single appearance on TV talent show *Opportunity Knocks* made 'Parrotface' comedian Freddie Davies famous overnight. Spectacular success followed, stars such as Judy Garland, Cliff Richard, even Cary Grant, were fans...

But when it all began to slip in the 1980s, Freddie became a producer and then forged yet another career as a serious actor. He appeared to great acclaim in a Royal Shakespeare Company production of *The Secret Garden* and cult film *Funny Bones* - alongside Lee Evans and Jerry Lewis - based on tales of Freddie's music hall comic grandfather Jack Herbert. Now he has come full circle, delighting audiences again as Samuel Tweet in theatres up and down the land.

Fifty years on from his television debut, Freddie finally tells his own story, revealing for the first time the tragedy behind his early days in Salford and a family secret that rocked his world. He paints a vivid and hilarious picture of a gruelling apprenticeship in the Northern clubs - revealing how 'Parrotface' spluttered into life.

With a foreword by the legendary Ken Dodd, this unique autobiography is a poignant and hilarious evocation of a vanished world, offering insights into the art of stand-up and a richly nostalgic treat for comedy connoisseurs.

Available in hardback or paperback

Headingley Ghosts

A collection of Yorkshire Cricket Tragedies

By Mick Pope

Compiled by Yorkshire cricket writer and researcher Mick Pope, *Headingley Ghosts* is a dark collection of over 60 Yorkshire cricket biographies, spanning more than 180 years of the game in the county. It has just been long-listed for the prestigious Cricket Society and MCC Book of the Year Awards, the winner of which will be announced at Lords in 2014.

From the Sheffield pioneers of the 1820s to the modern tragedy of David Bairstow, this haunting book - through original research and a wide selection of rare images - recalls what became of these tragic Yorkshire cricketers beyond the boundary.

They died young, they died old; they died in obscurity; they died in poverty; they died on the road, in the air and on the rail track; they died by their own hand; they died on the battlefields of war and sickness - collectively they are *Headingley Ghosts*.

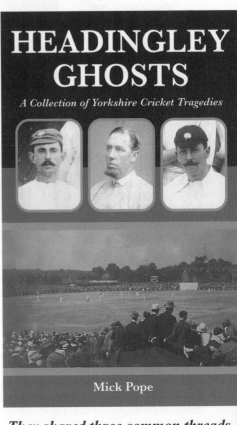

HEADINGLEY GHOSTS

A Collection of Yorkshire Cricket Tragedies

Mick Pope

They shared three common threads - Yorkshire, cricket and tragedy

The Barefoot Shepherdess

and Women of the Dales

By Yvette Huddleston & Walter Swan

The Barefoot Shepherdess and Women of the Dales celebrates the variety and versatility of a dozen or more determined women who have made a distinctive life for themselves "far from the madding crowd".

The Yorkshire Dales attracts tourists aplenty to appreciate the beauties of the local landscape but most visitors return to their towns and cities, renewed by the peace and quiet of the countryside, though unable to leave their modern, urban lifestyle for too long.

Women like Alison O'Neill, who owns her own flock of sheep and designs her own brand of tweed clothing, demonstrate that you can live a life of independence and fulfilment even in Britain's remotest regions. There are inevitable hardships to be endured but innumerable compensations when the Dales are on your doorstep.

Each chapter features inspirational women who have made the choice to live and work collaboratively with the people and places of the Yorkshire landscape. What they have in common - farmers, artists, vets, publicans, entrepreneurs, artisans, academics, curators and vicars - is a passion for life where Yorkshire countryside and community coincide.

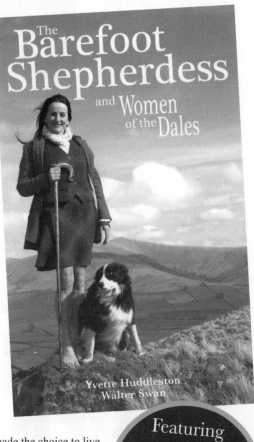

Featuring personalities from the ITV series **The Dales**

Through Adversity is the story of Damian Clayton MBE, whose relentless pursuit of the rugby league dream has seen him brush shoulders with royalty, tour the world, receive a gong in 2008 and be voted Combined Services Sports Official of the Year.

Despite having long since achieved his main goal - to see rugby league recognised officially by the Armed Forces - the inspirational Royal Air Force Flight Sergeant continues to give his all to the sport he loves.

Clayton, the RAF's 'Mr Rugby League', has been on a long journey. Since 1992 he has worked tirelessly to ensure the sport he has graced as player, administrator and coach is given the same official recognition that dozens of other sports that military personnel take part in - such as football, cricket and tennis - take for granted.

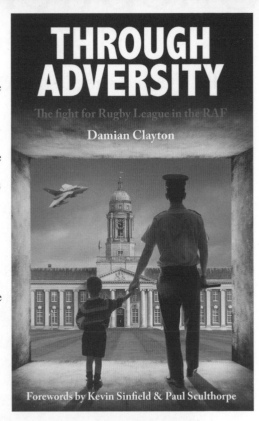

THROUGH ADVERSITY

The fight for Rugby League in the RAF

Damian Clayton

Forewords by Kevin Sinfield & Paul Sculthorpe

THROUGH ADVERSITY
By Damian Clayton MBE

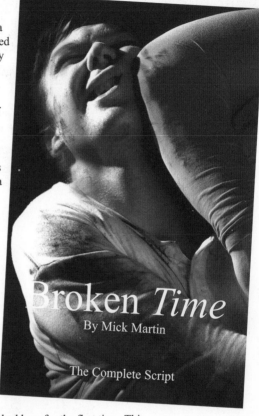

Investigate all our other titles and
stay up to date with our latest releases at
www.scratchingshedpublishing.co.uk